BLACK GODS OF THE METROPOLIS

BLACK GODS
OF THE METROPOLIS

NEGRO RELIGIOUS CULTS OF THE URBAN NORTH

By

ARTHUR HUFF FAUSET

UNIVERSITY OF PENNSYLVANIA PRESS

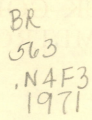

Copyright © 1944, 1971, by the
Trustees of the University of Pennsylvania

Originally published in 1944 as Volume III
of the Brinton Memorial Series, Publications
of the Philadelphia Anthropological Society.

First *Pennsylvania Paperback* edition published 1971

Library of Congress Catalog Card Number: 75-133446

ISBN: 0-8122-1001-8

PRINTED IN THE UNITED STATES OF AMERICA

INTRODUCTION

THERE is no more poorly understood area of Afro-American life than that of its churches, cults, and sects. Throughout the history of the black man in the United States, his churches have been the subject of fanciful speculation by scholars, sensationalists, reformers, entertainers, and bigots. All have seen these religious institutions in terms of their own preconceptions—as enemies of black liberation, as poor imitations of European religions, as static representations of the spiritual past of men, and so on.

The beginning point for understanding any religious institution is at least elementary knowledge of its practices and beliefs. But it is a sad fact that we have better descriptions—incomplete as they are—of religious beliefs and practices in West Africa, Brazil, and the Caribbean than we have of those of black people in the United States. And it is in this respect that *Black Gods of the Metropolis* is a singularly important book. Fauset, in writing one of the first books of urban American ethnography, took very seriously the culture of the Negroes of North America. Unfortunately, Afro-American cultural studies have proceeded very slowly since the original publication of this book, and so at least a few words on the problems of such studies are in order.

Fauset briefly mentions one of the central dilemmas of Afro-American studies when he considers the controversy that existed in the 1940's between the black sociologist E. Franklin Frazier and the white anthropologist Melville J. Herskovits.[1] It was Frazier's view that the African heritage of Negroes in North America had been virtually destroyed under the damaging experiences of slavery, and that the slave and his descendants came to embrace the white European's culture as a means of organizing and directing their experiences after Emancipation. Frazier further argued that a continual history of racial exclusion and dis-

---

1. The central sources for this debate are Melville J. Herskovits, *The Myth of the Negro Past*, (N.Y.: Harper and Bros.), 1941, and E. Franklin Frazier, *The Negro in the United States*, (N.Y.: Macmillan), 1949. For additional comment and references, see Norman E. Whitten, Jr. and John F. Szwed, eds., *Afro-American Anthropology: Contemporary Perspectives*, (N.Y.: Free Press), 1970, p. 28.

crimination combined with forced poverty (especially in northern cities) to prevent Negroes from ever fully achieving and stabilizing their newly learned culture. In other words, racism and poverty explain whatever differences exist between white and black cultural institutions and practices. Melville J. Herskovits, on the other hand, was hesitant to dismiss the African cultural heritage so quickly, particularly since he claimed to have discovered African parallels and retentions in the religion, language, kinship, music, and values of Afro-Americans in various parts of the West Indies and South America. For Herskovits, many differences between white and black cultural patterns could be explained by this continuity and reinterpretation of African cultures in the New World, and he argued that much of this continuity could be explained by the very practices of white racial exclusion and segregation to which Frazier drew attention. In short, Herskovits claimed that the black man, put in a position in which he could not share fully or continuously in American culture, kept what he wanted and could from his African background and remade a new culture to work for him in the Americas.

It would be appropriate at this point to review the merits of this controversy in light of the scholarly revelations which have emerged in the last thirty years. But the truth is that the question has not been given much serious thought, and very little has been contributed to it. Yet, without really being aware of the Frazier-Herskovits debate, most people today would probably hold views on the question quite similar to those argued by Frazier, for a wide spectrum now holds that racism and poverty are the sources of much of what has been called Afro-American culture, black ghetto culture, or even the culture of poverty. This is the view that one finds espoused in one form or another by such diverse commentators as Nathan Glazer and Daniel P. Moynihan, William H. Grier and Price M. Cobbs, Eldridge Cleaver and the Black Panther Party, Christopher Lasch, Oscar Lewis, and most educators, psychologists, and social workers.

This is not the place to attempt to reopen this controversy, even though it certainly merits reexamination. But it is wise to recall the findings of both Frazier's and Herskovits' work, and in doing so to realize that Afro-American societies, perhaps more so than most societies in the history of man, have been characterized by *both* continuity and discontinuity for just the reasons given by both Frazier and Herskovits. As Roger Bastide has argued, it is the special dialectic that exists between these two factors that should capture our interest and inform our research.

In this light, the problems involved in unraveling the story of Afro-American religions are difficult, but not impossible. The first step, of course, is just the one Fauset took in this book: to take Afro-American cultural behavior as it exists as the basic data from which to talk, and to see how it functions and serves in its many forms.[2] Minimally, this means relieving ourselves of the kind of ethnocentrism involved in concepts such as "escapism," "opiate," "charlatanry," and the like, which have passed as explanations so often in the past.

As suggested before, a second major problem in doing Afro-American cultural studies is the plain fact that we know far less about Afro-American history and culture than we do about that of either Africa or Europe. For example, in thinking about what Fauset calls the "unusual experiences" (spirit possession) characterizing four of the five cults in this book, we discover a poorly documented phenomenon of Afro-America, but one that is well described for Africa.[3] By concentrating on what little we do know of spirit possession among people of African descent in North America, it is possible to recognize the central position it has in many of their religious systems, as well as the patterned, cultural nature of these practices. Most commentators on possession in North America have in the past noted that some Euro-American people, especially in the American South, also practice spirit possession in their services, and thus have argued that the practice must have spread from white to black. The same arrogant logic would presumably attribute Afro-American contributions to American culture, such as jazz, baton twirling, black dialects, and black cuisine to Europe, simply because a large number of whites also practice them. Significantly, parallel forms of spirit posses-

---

2. Some recent writings on Afro-American cults and sects in North America include the following: Arthur H. Fauset, "Black Gods of the Metropolis," *Wayne State University Graduate Comment,* Vol. VII (No. 4, July, 1964), pp. 100-108; Martin Gelman, "Adat Beyt Moshe—The Colored House of Moses: A Study of a Contemporary Negro Religious Community and its Leader," unpublished Ph.D. dissertation, University of Pennsylvania, 1965; Helen L. Phillips, "Shouting for the Lord: A Black Rite of Modernization," unpublished M.A. thesis, University of North Carolina, 1969.; Kevan E. Simon, "A Grammar of the Mid-Week Service of the Church of the Living God," unpublished M.A. thesis, Temple University, 1968.

3. See, for example, John Beattie and John Middleton, eds., *Spirit Mediumship and Society in Africa,* (N.Y.: Africana Publishing Corp.), 1969.

sion exist in West Africa, Brazil, Jamaica, Trinidad, and Cuba, where it is clear that whites have learned black patterns and have even joined these black groups.

The evidence for the continuity, or more importantly, the reinterpretation and remodeling of African and early Afro-American traditions is compelling, and Fauset's accounts provide additional evidence. A few instances from Fauset's descriptions will have to suffice here, though it should be stressed that these are simply suggestions for further exploration, not final statements.

An example is the appellation "daddy" for one of the religious leaders of the cults discussed herein. It might be argued that this is simply an adaptation of Euro-American kinship terminology, but its widespread and varied usage among Afro-Americans should make us cautious. Early nineteenth century British and American sources tell us that the term was an address of endearment and recognition of accomplishment between English-speaking black males—and so it has remained in vernacular usage in America. This same term is used in similar religious cults in Jamaica and elsewhere in the Caribbean. The usual English etymological references tell us that "daddy" is ultimately derived from "baby talk," and certainly this may be the case, but as black English in Africa and the Americas has often been referred to as "baby talk," we might move even more cautiously. A further step would lead us to consider very similar words used in several African languages to indicate respect and formality, as well as fatherhood. Nothing about this is conclusive, but there is evidence that "daddy" implies something quite special among its users in these black cults, and that it represents an independent symbol in their system of religious ideas.

Still another example of this continuing modification of Afro-American traditions comes from the Moorish Science Temple of America and the Church of God, the least "African" of the groups that Fauset discusses. These are revitalistic groups, utopian in intent, both aiming at rejection of much of their own pasts, or at least the negative images of their pasts as imposed upon them by whites. Thus their lists of taboos include many of the behaviors that make up the negatively-valued stereotypes of Negroes as held by white men. One of these taboos—that against the eating of pork—at first glance would appear to be a simple adaptation of Islamic or Jewish custom. On the other hand, if one recognizes the importance of pork in the traditional cuisine of West Africans and Afro-Americans (along with chicken, their most valued

viii

meats), its tabooed nature becomes part and parcel of a larger rejection of their history. And with this is the possibility that the pig—like the spider and the rabbit before it—may have assumed the traditional role of trickster figure. In the vociferous rejection of a Muslim minister, for example, we find the following:

The hog is dirty, brutal, quarrelsome, greedy, ugly, foul, a scavenger which thrives on filth. It is a parasite to all other animals. It will even eat its own young. . . . In short, the hog has all the characteristics of the white man.[4]

If we remember the equation of the white man with the devil in Black Muslim cosmology, and we further recall the influence of ex-Muslim Malcolm X on young black militants such as the Panthers, we can better grasp the use of "pigs" to name policemen, of whom some, it is said, practice "trickification" on black people.

In the process of exploring Afro-American religions from this point of view, the object is not to search for "Africanisms" as simple survivals of African traditions—rather, the idea is to use Africa as a base line, in order to have a perspective from which to look. In the same way, the other Afro-American societies of Central and South America provide important points of comparison. Instead of simply searching out the *sources* of this or that pattern of behavior, we should concern ourselves with finding parallel processes and functions in African and Afro-American societies after European colonial and slavery contact. It is also worth remembering what Hortense Powdermaker pointed out long ago in *After Freedom,* her study of a Mississippi black community: that in taking on new cultural values from the white man, the black man did not simply replace older, "African" values, but he rather added newer patterns onto older patterns. This is what Paul Radin meant when he suggested that the "Negro was not converted to [the white Christian] God. He converted God to himself."[5] Both implied that African religious sensibilities were the starting place and that European religions were selectively adapted to the specialized needs of Afro-Americans. All of this is rather elementary anthropology, but in taking up the politically-frought subject of the roots and nature of Afro-American culture it is best

4. C. Eric Lincoln, *The Black Muslims in America,* (Boston: Beacon Press), 1961, p. 81.

5. Paul Radin, "Foreword" to *God Struck Me Dead,* Clifton H. Johnson, ed., (Philadelphia: Pilgrim Press), 1969, p. ix.

to remind ourselves of the universal principles that are shared by the most diverse groups of men.

The demands of Afro-American students for a cultural history that is relevant to black people—that is, one that includes both the distant and recent past of black people—have often been dismissed as lacking substance. Such dismissal depends primarily on the view that there is no unique Afro-American cultural past, only that of Africa, and that the connection between the two peoples is hard to draw. But works such as *Black Gods of the Metropolis* exist to put the lie to this, and thus deserve to be far better known. Though there have been many books on Afro-American history, Fauset's falls into the select group that includes works of Ralph Ellison, LeRoi Jones, and Albert Murray; that is, the writings of those who have best recognized the distinctiveness and power of Afro-American culture, and given it its proper place in the world.

JOHN SZWED

Philadelphia
July, 1970

AUTHOR'S NOTE TO
THE PAPERBACK EDITION

A FULL decade before Rosa Parks' tired feet focused a world spotlight on Montgomery, Alabama, and the Rev. Martin Luther King, this University of Pennsylvania study indicated the likely direction that future black religious leadership would take.

Many still assume that dependence on religion is a natural function of a black man's African heritage. E. Franklin Frazier and Robert E. Park dissented, and the present author concurs with them. The evidence still points to the fact that, African influence or no, the American black church "provided [the one] place where imaginative and dynamic blacks could experiment [without hindrance] in activities such as business, politics, social reform and social expression." It was stated additionally that the black church in America would likely "witness a transformation from its purely religious function to functions that will accommodate the urgent social needs of the black masses under stresses of politics and economics."

If anything the black church has exceeded the scope of this forecast. The Father Divine movement may properly lay claim to being a forerunner of the contemporary love-not-hate world movement. Their slogans are frequently identical; Father Divine's earlier-by-two-generations program even had its flower people (Rosebuds).

The Black Muslims are directly descended from the Moorish Science Temple. Elijah Muhumud, Muslim leader, stresses economic and cultural independence of blacks. Malcolm X became Elijah's disciple while serving a jail sentence; Eldridge Cleaver and many other recent black leaders became followers and proselytizers in this ostensibly religious movement. The tenuous thread, woven by Noble Drew Ali in long-ago tiny missions in Detroit, Chicago, and Newark, has penetrated the labyrinthine political maze all the way to the Black Panthers.

Truly those who ponder the future of our own great nation would do well to recall the aphorism, "Mighty oaks from tiny acorns grow."

ARTHUR HUFF FAUSET

New York City
July, 1970

CONTENTS

Chapter   *Page*

      INTRODUCTION   v

      AUTHOR'S NOTE   xi

   I   NEGRO RELIGIOUS CULTS IN THE URBAN NORTH   1

  II   MT. SINAI HOLY CHURCH OF AMERICA, INC.   13

 III   UNITED HOUSE OF PRAYER FOR ALL PEOPLE (BISHOP GRACE)   22

 IV   CHURCH OF GOD (BLACK JEWS)   31

  V   MOORISH SCIENCE TEMPLE OF AMERICA   41

 VI   FATHER DIVINE PEACE MISSION MOVEMENT   52

 VII   COMPARATIVE STUDY   68

VIII   WHY THE CULTS ATTRACT   76

 IX   THE CULT AS A FUNCTIONAL INSTITUTION   87

  X   THE NEGRO AND HIS RELIGION   96

 XI   SUMMARY OF FINDINGS   107

      APPENDICES   111

      BIBLIOGRAPHY   123

ILLUSTRATIONS

facing page

"Grace has given God a vacation . . ."   26
   (BISHOP GRACE)

Crossing over Jordan   27

"Holy Ghost, speak through me!"   62

"I have mastered the economic situation!"   63
   (FATHER DIVINE)

I

NEGRO RELIGIOUS CULTS IN THE URBAN NORTH

THE EMERGENCE OF THE NEGRO CULT

HARLEM is not the only "Negro city within a city." Philadelphia and Chicago both have Negro populations which exceed the total figures for such cities as Omaha and Richmond. Detroit and Cleveland are not far behind.

Most of the whites in these municipalities find reasons for by-passing the Negro districts. They see black folk only at a distance. Their genuine knowledge of these people is quite remote.

It is assumed, of course, that the lives of Negroes correspond to a pattern long made familiar and embellished in story and in song. They are said to be a carefree, happy-go-lucky folk, given to laughing and drinking, who resolve such troubles as they have in profound and seemingly uninterrupted experiences of religious emotionalism. Among many people who do not know Negroes very well, there is a general assumption that they are as predisposed toward the appeal of religion as fish are to water.

We shall leave to others a consideration of those questions involved in the general everyday living experiences of these Negro folk and confine ourselves to this single religious aspect. For the most part we shall be interested in only one phase of the religious life, namely, the influence of the so-called religious cult in the lives of some Negroes who inhabit certain sections of our large northern cities.

Anyone passing through one of these districts, especially at night, becomes aware of this influence. The signs are unmistakably present: frequently a store-front church, probably with improvised sign; the sound of tambourines, drums, wind and stringed instruments; the noise of unrestrained singing and shouting; and the dancing silhouettes. Sometimes the meeting place is more pretentious, and on occasion the ritual may be relatively subdued. The underlying pattern is fairly uniform, however, and it requires more than a few casual observations to detect

1

the fundamental differences which distinguish one group from another.

In this study we shall observe some of the practices prevailing among several representative groups of cult worshippers. It will be our purpose to probe beneath the merely superficial aspects of these practices in order to arrive at a deeper understanding of what is and has been taking place for many years among these Negroes in the development of their religious concepts and practices, under the modifying influences of new experiences in an American environment, especially in our great northern cities. At this point some historical perspective is in order.

It is safe to assume that not one Negro in the original cargo of slaves landed at Jamestown, Virginia, in 1619 was a member of the Christian faith. Probably less than a fraction of one per cent of the enormous numbers of Negroes who were victims of the slave traffic between Africa and the United States had any acquaintance with Christianity before their arrival on these shores.[1] It is quite remarkable, therefore, that less than one out of every hundred of the millions of Negroes in the United States today who adheres to a religious faith subscribes to any but a Christian belief, although practically all the Negroes living in America at this time are direct descendants of these African slaves whose religious background certainly was African and neither European nor Christian.

The influence of that overwhelming African heritage still must persist within the cultural nimbus which surrounds the religious beliefs and practices of the descendants of these African slaves. Yet the degree of that influence is problematical, to say the least, and is the subject of considerable dispute. In the earliest historical development of these practices among American Negroes the facts became obscured, partly because, for a considerable time, slave owners discouraged rather than encouraged the progress of Christianity among Negroes.[2] Consequently it is not until rela-

---

[1] W. E. DuBois, eminent scholar, states that "the total number of slaves imported is not known. Dunbar estimates that nearly 900,000 came to America in the sixteenth century, 2,750,000 in the seventeenth, 7,000,000 in the eighteenth, and over 4,000,000 in the nineteenth, perhaps 15,000,000 in all. Certainly it seems that at least 10,000,000 Negroes were expatriated. Probably every slave imported represented on the average five corpses in Africa or on the high seas." *The Negro*, p. 155.

[2] See G. R. Wilson, "Religion of the American Negro Slave," *Journal of Negro History*, VIII, 45: "They [the slaves] were handicapped in religious advancement because many owners believed that baptism made the slave free, which belief was prevalently held until 1729, when the Christian nations finally reached the decision that baptism did not mean manumission, and that even a Christian could be a slave."

tively late in the Negro's experience in the United States that we have trustworthy records of practices among Negro slaves which we may be certain are to be included within the general framework of their religious beliefs and practices. By this time the basic elements in these practices are frequently difficult to distinguish from those of various European forms, to which in large measure they undoubtedly owe their derivation.[3]

E. Franklin Frazier, a profound student of the origins of Negro institutions in America, is emphatic in his insistence that American religious practices owe very little to remote African influences. Thus, when referring to the rôle of the Negro preacher among the slaves, he says: "Undoubtedly, the most influential personalities among the slaves were the preachers. . . . These preachers became the interpreters of a religion which the slaves had developed on American soil. This religion was not a heritage, as many have assumed, from Africa."[4] He is in agreement with Park that various elements in the white man's religion "met the demands of his peculiar racial temperament and furnished relief to the emotional strains that were provoked in him by conditions of slavery."[5]

Wilson is of the opinion that "the religion of Africa disappeared from the consciousness of the American slave; that the slave himself, by contact with a new environment, became a decidedly different person, having a new religion, a primitive Christianity, with the central emphasis, not upon this world, but upon heaven."[6] He continues: ". . . the religion of the Negro slaves between 1619 and the Civil War did not originate in Africa, but was something totally different from the prevailing religion of the black continent."

Melville J. Herskovits probably ranks foremost among dissenters from this point of view. Granting a "partial validity" to the usual compensatory explanations of the special forms assumed

[3] Cf. Robert E. Park, "The Conflict and Fusion of Culture," *Journal of Negro History*, IV, 116: "Negro superstition is in no way associated, as it is in some of the countries of Europe . . . with religious beliefs and practices. It is not part of Negro Christianity. It is with him, as it is with us, folk-lore pure and simple."

Also cf. Wilson, *op. cit.*, p. 46: "With their various groups broken into fragments and scattered by the American slave trade, as the slaves here learned the English language, they were more able to assimilate the elements of Christianity found in American life. . . . Later as the whites saw that the Christian religion made the Negroes better slaves and did not set them free, the blacks secured more favorable opportunities for religious instruction."

[4] E. Franklin Frazier, *The Negro Family in the United States*, pp. 30–31.

[5] Park, *op. cit.*, p. 128.

[6] Wilson, *op. cit.*, p. 41.

by Negro versions of Christian dogma and ritual, he insists that the African influence, or at any rate the influence of the old African impulses, must definitely be taken into account in any appraisal of present-day American Negro religious forms and their derivation. "Underlying the life of the American Negro," he maintains, "is a deep religious bent that is but the manifestation here of a similar drive that, everywhere in Negro societies, makes the supernatural a major focus of interest." [7]

Expatiating upon the point, Herskovits continues:

The tenability of this position is apparent when it is considered how, in an age marked by skepticism, the Negro has held fast to belief. Religion is vital, meaningful, and understandable to the Negro of this country because . . . it is not removed from life, but has been deeply integrated into the daily round. It is because of this, indeed, that everywhere compensation in terms of the supernatural is so immediately acceptable to this underprivileged folk, and causes them, in contrast to other underprivileged groups elsewhere in the world, to turn to religion rather than to political action or other outlets for their frustration.

Whatever the remote influences on American Negro religious practices may or may not have been, there is quite general agreement with Frazier when he states, "It was only with the coming of the Methodists and Baptists that the masses of slaves found a form of Christianity that they could make their own." [8]

Certain it is that by the nineteenth century few American Negro slaves had failed to come under the influence of some kind of Christian religious instruction.

Usually, [says Joseph Brummell Earnest] on Sunday afternoons, but sometimes in the morning, the slaves would be gathered in the great house and lessons in the catechism had to be learned. The Apostles' Creed, the Lord's Prayer, and the Ten Commandments were also

---

[7] Melville J. Herskovits, *The Myth of the Negro Past*, p. 207.

[8] Frazier, *op. cit.*, p. 31. He quotes from Park, *op. cit.*, pp. 118–19. Herskovits agrees that the Baptist ritual and other influences in that church had a profound effect on American Negro religious practices, but he associates these influences with memories of the African past, particularly emphasizing the analogy between immersion in the Baptist church and certain African river rites. He says of African rites [of today]: ". . . in ceremony after ceremony . . . one invariable element [is] a visit to the river or some body of 'living' water, such as the ocean, for the purpose of obtaining the liquid indispensable for the rites. . . . The slaves . . . came to the United States with a tradition which found worship involving immersion in a body of water understandable, and encountered this belief among those whose churches and manner of worship were least strange to them. . . ." Herskovits, *op. cit.*, pp. 233–34.

taught. Hymns were sung and prayers rose to Heaven. Many good masters read sermons to their slaves. Other masters hired ministers. . . . Others preached themselves.[9]

It was not only Protestant denominations, however, that were instrumental in cultivating the slaves. Catholic missionaries also were active, although their activities in the United States did not in any degree compare with their efforts in Latin America.[10]

In the literature of the early development of Negro religious practices in North America there is scant evidence of dissensions over basic dogma and ritual. Presumably doctrinal disputes caused relatively little concern, and resultant splits seem to have been rare. At first the Episcopal and Presbyterian churches, both in the North and South, made efforts to win over Negro converts; but for various reasons the bulk of the Negroes preferred to go over to the Baptist and Methodist denominations.

Questions and disputes did arise, however; but most of the disputations referred to the attitudes of whites, who sought in one way or another to make distinctions between Negroes and whites in their places of worship. At the same time there developed among many Negroes a consciousness of the need for greater expression in the church through Negro leadership. This the white leadership frequently was reluctant to encourage, although it sometimes happened that the white leaders were willing to assist Negroes in establishing churches of their own where Negro leadership would have an opportunity to develop to the fullest.[11]

The most important effect of these separatist tendencies was to establish among Negroes all over the United States the habit of worshipping apart from other Christians. Thus vast religious institutions, collateral with the white bodies but almost exclu-

[9] Joseph Brummell Earnest, *The Religious Development of the Negro in Virginia*, p. 60.

[10] *Negro Year Book, 1937–38*, pp. 228–34, and John W. Cromwell, "First Negro Churches in the District of Columbia," *Journal of Negro History*, VII, 102–6. The most authoritative and complete study is the recently published work by John T. Gillard, *Colored Catholics in the United States*.

[11] However, it also happened frequently, especially in the South, that Negroes were not permitted to worship separately, if at all, for fear that the place and time of worship would be utilized by the Negroes to plot slave rebellions. There were many such revolts, sometimes involving much bloodshed. The most notable were those led by Denmark Vesey in South Carolina, 1822, and by Nat Turner in Virginia, 1831. The slavocracy's fear of the potentialities of the slave situation resulted in stringent efforts on their part to procure state laws forbidding Negroes to congregate for any purpose. For details of these and similar rebellions, consult Herbert Aptheker and Carter G. Woodson, noted in Bibliography.

sively Negro in their corporeal structure if not in inspiration, developed and flourished. The Negro church thereby became an instrument of, by, and for Negroes.[12]

The desire for freer self-expression than was possible in the prevailing white churches, plus an insistence on the part of certain Negroes, especially in the North, that the Christian philosophy of the universal brotherhood of man must include Negroes, did much to foster the separation which began to develop between white and Negro worshippers. An additional spur to the gradual, almost complete, emancipation of Negro worship from white influence was the conflict over slavery which raged within the white church itself. The paradox of a church torn to the point of schism between pursuit of the dollar and adherence to humanitarian principles did not escape the attention of Negro worshippers. Their faith was sorely tried.

Particularly in Philadelphia and other northern centers, Negroes fought vigorously against segregation in church edifices and against other forms of racial discrimination. In numerous instances the differences of the Negro dissenters assumed the proportions of a revolt. Out of such storms in the North and the acrimonious attitudes engendered among southern whites by the slave controversy, together with the natural inclination of many Negroes to develop independently, came the Negro church as we know it today. Within a period of half a century after the American Revolution, great Negro religious denominations, including the African Methodist Episcopal, the African Methodist Episcopal Zion, and the Negro Baptist church, as well as other denominations catering to smaller numbers of Negroes, had been established.

Thus the American Negro church represents the one institution among Negroes in the United States where we are privileged to observe the seeds of revolt, so inherent in the institution of

[12] Curiously, the denomination which was to have relatively the least influence among the Negroes, namely the Catholic, is the only one of the important denominations which has rarely encouraged the idea of separate status between white and Negro worshippers. This may be the result of the paucity of Negro communicants rather than a policy which is unique from the point of view of customary historical development in American life. (Of the total Negro population 2.3 per cent (296,998) is Catholic according to Gillard, *op. cit., supra.*) Recently a split has developed in this church also, and a group of Negroes have formed a Catholic sect known as the African Orthodox Church, with branches in New York City, Philadelphia, and other centers. The reason for this split, I am informed by one of the priests of the sect, is that under the Roman Catholic church Negro priests were not granted all rights implied in the priestly office.

slavery, taking root and sprouting. Indeed, the American Negro church, viewed historically, provides numerous vivid examples of the Negro's capacity to revolt.[13]

In the twentieth century a noticeable concern with doctrine and ritual appears to distinguish the attitude of many Negro churchgoers who formerly were more interested in the problem of maintaining the old established churches in a flourishing condition. With the migration of Negroes from the rural South to urban centers, a transformation in the basic religious life and attitudes also is observable. The church, once a *sine qua non* of institutional life among American Negroes, does not escape the critical inquiry of the newer generations, who implicitly and sometimes very explicitly are requiring definite pragmatic sanctions if they are to be included among churchgoers, or if indeed they are to give any consideration at all to religious practices and beliefs.

As Ira Reid points out:

There are indications that a new church is arising among Negroes, a militant church, one that is concerning itself with the problems of the masses. Sometimes it is the old-line Protestant church, sometimes a younger denomination, sometimes a Catholic congregation— and sometimes a community church. Its leaders organize and take part in aggressive social movements for the public and the race's weal. Led, in a few urban and rural centers, by outstanding men who are trained and practiced in religious thought as well as in economics, this church is vital. Yet it cannot be said that today even this church is an influential factor in the lives of the whole Negro working population. Extremely significant in Negro life, however, has been the inordinate rise of religious cults and sects. Even before the depression one noted this tendency. . . . Today, Father Divine, Daddy Grace, Moslem sects, congregations of Black Jews and the Coptic Church, have been added to the church organizations existing among Negroes. Their influence and reach are enormous and significant— perhaps more socially adapted to the sensationalism and other unique characteristics of city life, and the arduousness and bitter realities of race, than the prayerful procrastinations of the church institutions they now supplant.[14]

[13] See Carter G. Woodson, *The Education of the Negro Prior to 1861, The History of the Negro Church, The Negro in Our History.* Also numerous volumes of the *Journal of Negro History;* and Richard Allen, *The Life of Richard Allen,* Charles H. Wesley, *Richard Allen, Apostle of Freedom;* likewise, Benjamin Elijah Mays and Joseph William Nicholson, *The Negro's Church.*

[14] Ira De A. Reid, *In a Minor Key,* pp. 84–85.

In this study we shall subject to scrutiny five of these special groups, or "cults," as Reid calls them.   We shall touch upon their origins in America, including in some instances the character and life history of their founders; observe their organizational forms; and witness their practices, rituals, and attempts to achieve their objectives.   We shall note some of the characteristics which distinguish them one from another and from other denominations which are more representative of the "old time religion," and we shall see how they function.

At this point it is in order to note some of the questions raised by the presence of these cults in our great northern centers, as well as to lay down our general methodological procedure in observing them.

WHAT DO THE CULTS MEAN?

We have observed how large groups of Negroes in the United States, after having accepted the basic tenets of European Christianity, almost exclusively in its Protestant form, broke away from the established white churches to form churches of their own. The chief reasons for these separatist tendencies were the reluctance of white Christians to accept Negroes in the already established churches on a plane of equality, and the desire of Negroes to worship in churches where they could feel free to express themselves along the lines which the general condition of their lives prompted.

By the time of Emancipation numerous denominations had been created among the Negroes, most of them duplicating in black the prevailing white prototypes.   Gradually after the Civil War these denominations grew larger in size and more powerful in their influence among the Negroes.

About the beginning of the twentieth century, possibly co-existent with the industrial and economic upheaval which was characterizing the same period, new types of Negro churches made their appearance.   These more nearly represented *doctrinal* splits within the older established models.   These splits took names like "Holiness," [15] "Church of God," "Apostolic," etc., thereby

---

[15] In this study "holiness" churches comprise those sects which require the following experiences before an individual can be said to be a true member or to have been "saved":

1. Conversion
2. Sanctification (leading a pure life)
3. Spirit possession (filled with the Holy Spirit).

When one is converted, he turns from the sins of the world and concentrates upon

testifying to their essentially Christian or Judaic motivation.

Later and further developments in the tendency to form splits show pronounced "nationalistic" characteristics, that is, churches which tend to emphasize the racial qualities of the communicants, sometimes almost to the exclusion of any preoccupation with the Deity, the Christ, or the Trinity.

Raymond Julius Jones has classified these cults in the United States as follows:

1. Faith Healing
2. Holiness
3. Islamic (a broader classification would be "nationalistic")
4. Pentecostal
5. Spiritualist.[16]

The five cults included in the present study will be found to fall within this classification with the exception of "spiritualistic," which I purposely have excluded as being not primarily characteristic of, or especially significant among, the religious practices of the Negro people of the United States. (According to the figures of the *Negro Year Book, 1937–38,* a total of seventeen urban spiritualistic churches throughout the United States had a membership of less than one thousand.)

In any northern metropolitan area it will be possible to discover various examples of most of these types. For consideration in this volume, I have selected the following cults:

Mt. Sinai Holy Church of America, Inc. (Types 1–2–4) [17]
United House of Prayer for All People (1–2–4)
Church of God (Black Jews) (3–2–1)
Moorish Science Temple of America (3)
Father Divine Peace Mission Movement (1–2)

These particular cults have been selected not only because they afford an opportunity to observe the range of contemporary cult practice among urban Negroes in the United States, but also be-

---

"spiritual" values. If the conversion is genuine, it should result in living a pure life (sometimes called "holy," "evangelical," "sanctified"). In due time an unusual experience is bound to occur. This may be a vision, a dream, a miraculous healing, a sudden impulse to utter strange sounds, unintelligible to all but the person making the utterance (commonly known as "speaking in tongues"), or some other exceptional happening.

16 *A Comparative Study of Religious Cult Behavior among Negroes with Special Reference to Emotional Group Conditioning Factors.*

17 Usually in these churches there is considerable typological overlapping. The figures refer to the types as given in the Jones classification, above.

cause for the metropolitan areas referred to these are among the most important and best-known cults of their respective types, and hence among the most representative. Most of our data have been taken from observations made in the city of Philadelphia, but in some instances, particularly in the case of the Father Divine Peace Mission Movement, data obtained in New York City and elsewhere are included.

Although the tendency of Negro religious cults to spread in the large northern centers has been marked during the past two decades, still the aggregate number of cult members in these centers does not represent a sufficiently large proportion of the total Negro population to warrant more than tentative generalizations; this fact must be borne in mind constantly in a consideration of the data contained in this study. Nevertheless, the number of cult worshippers is substantial and appears to be increasing. Therefore it would be as grave an error to discount the significance of the presence of the cults as it would be to overestimate their importance.[18] Undoubtedly the cults are able to shed light on some of the questions concerning the Negro and his religious attitudes to which reference has already been made.

Both Herskovits [19] and Park [19] have raised the question of the predisposition of the Negro toward religion and certain forms of religious attitudes. Therefore we shall be interested to note whether observations among these cults further substantiate their speculations.

We shall of course be interested in the question which Herskovits has revived: "Does contemporary religious practice among Negroes in the United States disclose definite African survivals?" Do the cults under observation indicate "Negro" form and "Negro" content in the practices now prevalent among them, rather than "American" or "European" form and content as students like Frazier and Wilson are inclined to believe? [20]

---

[18] In Mays's and Nicholson's study (*op. cit.*) the Baptist and Methodist denominations shared approximately 60 per cent of the number of churches in Philadelphia. Holiness churches alone were accountable for 20 per cent (considerably higher than the Methodist); the remaining 20 per cent was shared by all other denominations, which included, of course, other cult groups. Granted that some of the individual Methodist and Baptist church organizations have memberships which equal many times the membership of some of the individual store-front churches of the cults, nevertheless it can be seen that the cults are a factor in the religious life of Philadelphia.

[19] *Op. cit.*

[20] While no attempt has been made in this study to identify cult members according to their places of birth, from time to time samplings were made. The frequency of southern birth, usually in the Deep South, is high.

Since Frazier, Park, Wilson, and many others are of the opinion that Negro religion in America is little more than an adaptation of European Christianity to the American Negro's need to compensate for social, physical, and economic conditions in America, we shall scrutinize the evidence for indications of functional expressions (as against "pure" African survivals) destined to transform certain social needs of the American Negro folk into cultural necessities and imperatives which are derived from their cultural milieu.

Finally, borrowing a suggestion from Reid,[21] we shall observe some of the avenues into which these practices have been directed, assuming, as Reid intimates, that the cults do have the great significance which their rapid and increasing spread in urban communities would seem to indicate.

In obtaining the data utilized in this study, the author spent a period of more than two years making scores of visits to the places of worship, as well as to the homes of numerous members and leaders of the various cults. The study suffers from the obvious disadvantage that in no case could the author be identified as a member of any of the cults under consideration, and consequently his approach to members always had to be that of an outsider, even in those instances where he was accepted as a trusted friend of members and leaders.

In some instances, because he was not a member, it has been difficult almost to the point of impossibility to learn some of the facts which would be desirable in a study of this kind. This is notably true in the case of the Moorish Science Temple, whose members are most taciturn to all outsiders, even to those whom they regard as friends. This cult is in reality a secret organization, whose principles are not to be divulged publicly, and whose general purposes, ritual, and intimate practices ordinarily are shielded from the gaze of outsiders, particularly members of the white group. I have been careful in my treatment of this cult not to tell everything that has come to my attention because I realize that to do so would be considered an unpardonable breach of trust against members of the cult who made me a confidant.[22]

---

[21] Reid, *op. cit.*, pp. 84–85.

[22] Since the beginning of the Second World War, efforts have been made to link the Moors with various subversive efforts. Not only is the present Prophet Noble Drew Ali, Reincarnated, very emphatic on the subject of loyalty to the United States Government, but in all my visits to meetings of the Moors I never heard a single subversive utterance. The *Koran* of the cult specifically preaches loyalty to the United States, and in the temple the American flag is always conspicuous.

In general, the method of approach to these cults has been to visit a place of worship frequently enough to become accepted as a friendly spectator and participant in the rites.   From this point it has been possible to establish cordial relations with members and leaders who usually are only too willing to spend time with a stranger in order to impress upon him the virtues of their particular form of worship.

On numerous occasions it was not possible to take down verbatim transcriptions of conversations and performances, since these occurred under conditions where it would have been improper or impolitic to be seen making obvious notes.   Where case histories are given, however, it was possible, either at the place of worship or at the worshipper's home or place of occupation, to arrange for taking notes on the spot.   Since usually, even in the case histories, notes are the product of a single though frequently protracted conversation with the informant or informants, there still remains the need for investigations of a more extended type by students who will be able in a more sustained relationship with the cult members to identify themselves more intimately with the groups under study.

In presenting the testimonies and case histories of members of the cults, an attempt has been made to preserve as nearly as possible the manner and form of the material as presented by the informants.

Also, because the various aspects of cult life appear to have achieved a higher degree of development in the Father Divine Peace Mission Movement than in any of the other cults studied, it has been given a somewhat more extended treatment.   Finally, it should be borne in mind that the materials and other data in this study usually bear a date not later than the year 1941.   It is conceivable that some modifications of form, if not of content, have taken place since the beginning of the War.   These changes, we are sure, will be found to be limited in scope, requiring little or no modification of the general outlines of this presentation.[23]

23 Two such changes are the removal of the Philadelphia temple of the Moorish Science Temple of America from Lombard Street to Eighteenth Street, north of Christian, and the transfer by Father Divine of his principal offices from New York City to Philadelphia.

II

MT. SINAI HOLY CHURCH OF AMERICA, INC.

TESTIMONY OF J. H.[1]

MY wife and I were Baptists. My wife got zealous because she said she wanted to get nearer to the holy spirit and so she joined with Mt. Olive. That put my wife a step higher in Christianity than I was. This was not so good. So I studied and interviewed the holy people in order to even up things. One thing I noticed. Before my wife went into Mt. Sinai, she was always ill. She couldn't have children. She always got very sick when she was pregnant, and we would lose the child and we would be about to lose her. So she was pregnant along about the time she went into the holiness church. She knew she was due to get ill but she said she had the holiness now, and she was going to have the faith to keep her from getting ill. She said she wasn't going to have no doctor, she wasn't going to no hospital, nothing like that. And sure enough she didn't go to no hospital, and the only time she had the doctor was round about the time to have the baby, and she had the baby, and everything was all right. And for sixteen years after she joined Mt. Sinai, until she died, she was never sick. Well, I interviewed the holy people. Because of the strictness of some of their rules I didn't agree with everything, but I got ready to join. And I was with them for ten years. And there was a funny thing with me. I worked for a company where I got paid on the first and the fifteenth of the month. But in order to draw a full month's pay I always had to dose up on Feenamint, Black Draught, or something like that. But ten years ago, through faith on account of the faith of my wife, I got the faith also, and if you were to go up in my closet now, I guess you would find the remains of that bottle of medicine where I left off at that time, and I haven't needed any ever since.

ORIGIN

Although the members of the Philadelphia branch of the Mt. Sinai Holy Church frequently refer to it as Mt. Sinai, the branch name is really Mt. Olive. The Mt. Sinai Holy Church of America, Inc. is composed of many such branches throughout the United States.

---

[1] Additional testimonies of the various cult members are to be found in Appendix A.

The founder of the church, Bishop Ida Robinson, was born in Florida. She grew up in Georgia. At the age of seventeen she was converted and began churchwork. Soon she left the South and came to Philadelphia, where she founded the Mt. Sinai Holy Church in 1924. Since that time she has ordained a vice-bishop, Elmira Jeffries, and numerous elders, preachers, etc.

Bishop Robinson is tall, sharp of feature and eye, medium brown in color, probably of mixed Indian-Negro blood. Her education has been limited, but she is extremely intelligent, and a competent leader. She is, of course, a keen student of the Bible.

ORGANIZATION

The Philadelphia church is located at Oxford Street, east of Twenty-Second. Formerly it was the property of a white Pentecostal congregation now located at Nineteenth and Green streets, Philadelphia. The main meeting room of the church is on the second floor, but there are meeting rooms on the first floor also, and here many of the weekday meetings are held.

Mt. Sinai is distinctive among the cults considered here in the extent and degree of female participation. Many of the elders are women, as are also a large number of the preachers. In addition, however, there are many men in official places.

Bishop Ida Robinson, the founder of the cult, is the supreme head. Her authority is said to come directly from God.

Vice-Bishop Elmira Jeffries is her immediate assistant. Next below her is Elder Mary E. Jackson, who is known as Secretary of the corporation.

In each of the cities where there is a member church, there is a presbyter or an elder who is appointed by the bishop. These presbyters form what is known as a board of presbyters, and these nominally govern the church, though Bishop Robinson is the final authority.

Each individual member church has its own board of elders, and the ordinary members are known as brothers and sisters.

In order that all the member churches may have a chance to compare notes, join together in formulating policy, renew the spirit of holiness, elect elders, etc., each year there is a convocation of all branches.

MEMBERSHIP

While the church is open to any person who might wish to join, membership is granted only to those who have satisfied the elders of the church that they are worthy to be called into the fold. A tentative membership is acknowledged on the basis of conversion; but full membership comes only after a period of testing, which is known as sanctification, and an experience, usually speaking in tongues, which is the sign that one has been filled with the Holy Spirit. There is no such thing as "bringing a letter" from another church; and of course no recognition is given to past membership in one of the orthodox churches. Membership must be passed upon by the elders of the church, and these same elders always reserve the right to abrogate that membership for cause.

After one has become a brother or sister, he may apply to become a member of the Preachers' Class. Here the neophyte preachers are drilled in Bible lore and spiritual wisdom according to the light of holiness in order that they may be able to expound holiness wherever they may be sent. In Philadelphia this class meets on Wednesday nights under the direction of Elder Jackson. Usually its members sit in a body during church services; frequently they worship in a body, which is to say, they will rise in unison, sing, dance, or shout in unison.

FINANCE

The main financing of the church is through the collection of tithes, which are rigidly exacted. In addition there are numerous collections during the services, including passing the collection plates and marching to the table. If a visiting preacher participates in the services, it is customary to "lift" a special offering for him.

A favorite method of drawing members to the collection table is for the bishop to march down from the pulpit, through the main body of the church and thence back to the collection table which is at the front of the church. Numbers of her followers will march behind her and place their offerings on the table.

There is a board of deacons which accounts for all collections except the tithes which are accounted for solely by Bishop Robinson and Elder Jackson. (This refers to the Philadelphia church.)

Concerts and similar ventures are also held for the raising of funds.

SACRED TEXT

The sacred text is the Bible.

BELIEFS

It is necessary first to be converted in order to become a member of the church.   Then one must be sanctified or purified by living a holy and evangelical life; and finally one must be filled with the Holy Spirit.

Conversion is equivalent to conception: the seed has been implanted.   ("Ye must be born again.")

Sanctification is equivalent to gestation: it is necessary that a person be sanctified by the Blood of the Lamb before he can be born into the church.   The proof of a person's rebirth is that he no longer sins.

God has ordained four types of human beings:

1. The elect—even before they were born, they had been chosen by God.
2. The compelled—these could not help themselves from being saved.
3. The "whosoever will"—these can be saved if they choose.
4. The damned—these are ordained for Hell.

A member must be baptized in the name of the Father, the Son, and the Holy Ghost.

All leading members believe in spiritual healing.   This belief is encouraged because it is rooted in faith in God as healer.   He can, however, heal only those who have implicit faith in His power to heal; therefore if there is the least doubt, a physician should be called or use made of ordinary remedies.   But if a vow to be healed only through the spirit of God has been taken, then a member is bound to refuse medicine or to have a physician.

The following are sins against the condition of sanctification: fornication, adultery, lying, stealing, backbiting, straightening the hair, impure conversation, swearing, participation in athletic games, attendance at football, baseball games, etc., drinking intoxicants, smoking, polishing the nails, wearing short dresses, attending motion pictures, chewing gum, gambling in any form, visiting parks like Coney Island or Woodside.

RITUAL

Typical Service

The members are seated in the meeting room.   In the absence of the head of the church or her representative there may or may not be a leader.   While they wait the group is held together by communal singing (usually spontaneous), accompanied by much clapping of the hands; usually a piano also accompanies the singing.

After a song, a member will testify somewhat as follows:

I am happy to be present in the Lord's house this night.   The Lord has been my rock and my guide all during the week.   I would be a weak vessel except for the Lord, and I thank God that He has kept me holy and pure ever since the great day I entered this church.   I was a very sick woman last week, but I just thought on the Lord and He touched me with His healing power.   Since then I haven't had any more headache or misery in the stomach.   Pray for me, sisters and brothers, that I may remain holy and sanctified, pure in the faith, now and forever, Amen.

Usually each testimony is followed by a song by the group, but it sometimes happens that several members testify between songs. When fervor becomes intense two or more members will occasionally testify simultaneously.   Sometimes penny collections interrupt the singing and testifying.   The meeting goes on in this manner until the preacher arrives.

After the arrival of the preacher, the singing becomes more intense, and usually the preacher takes charge of it.   Since by this time the greater proportion of the congregation will have arrived, a collection for the general welfare of the church may be taken.   This does not preclude the possibility of numerous other collections, usually of the penny variety, for various purposes.

The preacher proceeds to expound a sermon on a subject such as "What Time Is It?"   She predicts that we are approaching the millennium (year 2000) and therefore it is nearly twelve o'clock midnight in the eternal scheme of time.   It is very dark, because the darkest hours are just before the dawn.   This means that the worst sins are going on.   So she rails against backbiting, numbers playing, gum-chewing, adultery, lying, stealing.   There is constant reference to adultery, to the sin of looking upon another with a lustful eye.   It is getting close to time, and unless you are born again, i. e., conceived anew, the millennium will arrive and you will be among the damned.   All during the sermon there is much shouting, "Amen!   Praise the Lord!", etc., and from time to time the preacher interrupts her discourse with a song which is taken up by the congregation.   If the preacher senses that her words are not getting over, or that there is a lassitude creeping over the congregation, she will cry out, "Help me!" or she will

plead, "Holy Ghost, speak through me!" At various times during the sermon a single member or a group of members will rise
suddenly and speak in tongues and perhaps dance about either
in place or through the hall. If the member is too violent, or
seems likely to harm herself or some other members, less affected
brothers and sisters will restrain her, with gentle admonitions if
these will suffice, otherwise forcibly. Sometimes it is necessary
to draw a human cordon around the individual to make sure she
does not get out of hand. The sermon varies in length, sometimes being relatively brief, twenty minutes to a half hour, at
other times an hour or more. When the sermon ends, usually
with a song rather than a spoken prayer, the preacher may sit
down and relax after the strenuous performance, or she may start
at once to take up the collection (it may be made by one of the
elders), stepping down from the rostrum and leading the proces-
sion through the church and down the aisle to the collection
table, singing and exhorting and calling for liberal contributions.

One service merges immediately into another. When the
preacher considers that the service of which she was the main
feature has been concluded, she may leave the room or she may
sit quietly on the rostrum and look on at another service, such
as a young people's meeting, a special service by one of the clubs
to commemorate a birthday, or merely to raise funds.

If it is the first Sunday of the month the preacher will leave
for several hours while subsidiary services are conducted prepara-
tory to the communion service which occurs about 5 P.M. Some
of this time will be taken up in the inevitable testimonial meeting, with the customary shouting, dancing, and, rarely, rolling
on the floor.

Meanwhile some officers of the church are setting up tables for
the communion service. At about five o'clock the bishop returns
to begin the service. The tables are stretched across the front
of the room. The bishop sits in the middle, facing the congregation, and on either side of her sit male and female elders.
Other elders, deacons, and deaconesses stand behind her.

The service begins with the blessing of infants and little children who are brought up to the bishop by their parents. The
bishop takes them into her arms, one by one, and pronounces a
blessing, usually adding some remark calculated to make the older
folk laugh.

After this ceremony has been completed, everybody in the
church is welcomed to the communion table where grape juice

and crackers are served. Various members proceed to the table and seat themselves facing the officers, their own backs to the congregation. The first to be served are the officers of the church. The ceremony is conducted with amazing rapidity, one group arising quickly from the table to make room for the next group of communicants. The choir is the last to be served, for it has been singing lustily during the whole service, accompanied by piano, drum, cymbals, and the constant handclapping of singers.

After the communion service has been ended, there still remains the rite of symbolic foot-washing. Water is sprinkled from a basin on the bare foot, and dried with a towel. Women attend women, and men attend men. During this ceremony, too, there is singing and dancing, but it is noticeable by the time the last communicants are having their feet washed that the congregation has dwindled to a bare handful of people. There is an informal air about the church such as one observes at a theatre as the last few patrons straggle out. Members of the church, however, are merely leaving temporarily in order to obtain food and refreshment before the evening service, which will soon follow.

PRACTICES

Divorce is taboo.

When a person asks to become a member of the church, his marital status and sex relationships must be rigidly scrutinized.

Marriage must be within the group, but if one is a married person before he or she enters the group, he will not be excluded even though his spouse does not choose to enter with him.

If a married couple are members of the cult, and for some reason one of them leaves the group, then the other member must either leave the cult or separate from his spouse.

A remarkable instance of the rigidity of the sex rules is demonstrated in the following case of Elder Z.: [2] Some years before Elder Z. joined Mt. Sinai she had been married to a man in a distant city. Subsequently the two had separated. Later, Elder Z. learned from her husband's mother that he had died; at least his mother was quite certain of his death because she had not seen or heard from him in a long time, and lately she had had a dream in which she saw his corpse. Some time after this, Elder Z. and another man fell in love. At that time both of them were mem-

[2] The language employed in this example closely follows that of the informant.

bers of the Methodist church. They married and lived "sweetly" together in that church. Then they came to Philadelphia. There they joined Mt. Sinai Holy Church, and both became elders. But one day, as Elder Z. was walking along the street, she spied a man on a trolley car who bore a striking resemblance to her former husband. Her mind was troubled. She was determined to make sure on the question, and had the man located. Then she visited him. Sure enough, it was her former husband. She went to her second husband and confided the facts to him. They did not hesitate, but approached the elders of their church and the bishop, with the result that it was decided among them that the two should separate. Both spouses were quick to agree, because although they were greatly devoted to each other, they knew that they would be committing intentional adultery if they remained steadfast, and this would exclude them both from heaven. There was no question of annulling the former marriage because the church does not permit divorce. As a result, the two still are in the church, working intimately and lovingly together, but living separately as if they never had had a moment of closer association.

In connection with marriage practices, the following instance is pertinent: An elder in the Philadelphia church announced that he desired to marry a woman who was a member of the Baptist church. He sought a dispensation for this. It was refused. He married the woman notwithstanding, and was compelled to resign from the board of elders, and subsequently had to drop his membership in the cult.

Men and women must show no sentiment toward each other unless they plan to marry. This applies especially to boys and girls. (This rule has been relaxed because of the difficulty of enforcing it.)

Women must "dress holy," that is their dresses must be severely plain, skirts long, stockings preferably of cotton, and black or white in color. Short dresses are forbidden.

Beautification of the person is taboo.

Among men, a sign of holiness is not to wear a necktie; should a necktie be worn it must be either plain white or black.

Speaking in tongues is essential.

One must prove that he has had a supernatural experience (spirit possession), otherwise he may not become a member.

The rites of baptism, communion, and foot-washing are observed.

During services it frequently happens that all members get on their knees and pray aloud simultaneously, each person saying his own prayer.

There are various auxiliaries, such as clubs, for raising money. These moneys are used to feed the poor, to maintain schools similar to public schools, and for other philanthropic purposes.

There are visitation committees for attending the sick, giving money to or feeding the sick, reading scripture to ill members, etc.

III

UNITED HOUSE OF PRAYER FOR ALL PEOPLE

I LIVED in Raleigh, North Carolina. I had been a Methodist for twenty-seven years, but I really didn't know what the spirit of the Lord truly meant. I thought I knew, but I never had any experience like I got after I saw the light. It was like this: I had been going to the Methodist church, but Bishop Grace came through Raleigh. He performed miracles of healing. All kinds of people were healed. There was a blind woman. She couldn't see a thing for five years, but Daddy Grace set up his tent and she came to his meeting and he touched her. I saw her healed right on the spot. She jumped way up in the air after he healed her. And there were three blind men. He healed them the same way. And I was healed in 1925. I had the sinus something terrible for five years, ever since 1920. The doctors said they cured me but they didn't. The pains were awful, all down my face, through my nose; it was like a sharp knife cutting through, and all in my eyes and the back of my head. It was awful misery, and nothing they told me to do stopped it. But Bishop Grace laid his hands on me, and all that pain left me completely. But I didn't join his House of Prayer yet. He didn't have any place in Raleigh. It was in Charlotte in 1929, and I was going to Dr. Garr's tabernacle. I was listening to Dr. Garr, and all of a sudden I had a vision. It was this man Grace. He appeared to me from the right side, just about a foot in front of me. He didn't say anything but I knew then I should follow him. Pretty soon he came to Charlotte. He was staying at Sister Sallie Hill's house on Hill Street in Charlotte. We all went over to see him at Sister Hill's home, me and my whole family. They were sitting in the back and I was standing in the doorway. All of a sudden I fell dead. I died, fell dead in the doorway. But Bishop Grace put his hand on my chest and right away it was like an electric shock passing through me. I quivered and shook all over and my right arm just rattled against the wall. I got up right then and there, and I have never had a doctor since 1929. I joined the House of Prayer then and my whole family and I have been members ever since. We help him to build other houses of prayer. We're helping him here in Philadelphia. There isn't any leader except Grace. There isn't any religion except through Grace. Grace can heal you.

[1] See also Appendix A.

When he puts the *Grace Magazine* on your chest, it is the healing power of the spirit. Look up Ezekiel 47:12. It speaks of a tree and says the leaf shall be medicine. The same in Revelations 22:2. The *Grace Magazine*, that is from the leaf; that is why it can heal, and I have seen it heal all kinds of sickness. Every book in the Bible has been sealed by Grace. All through the Bible there is Grace. If you don't believe it, just look up Genesis 6:8, or Luke 2:40, and Titus 2:11, and Ephesians 2:7–8, and Ephesians 4:7, and all through the Old and New Testaments. Grace is the greatest thing in the world today. Grace will bring you through.

ORIGIN

The founder of this cult, Bishop Charles Emmanuel Grace, is a man of mixed parentage, said to be Negro and Portuguese. Bronze of color, and with flowing hair, he does not admit to being a Negro. Frequently he adopts a patronizing attitude towards his Negro followers (who in Philadelphia and New York represent nearly 100 per cent of the members) by pointing out to them that when he took on earthly form he chose to lead the Negroes, lowly in state though they are, rather than the members of some more privileged racial group.

This church had its origin in the South where, according to reports, Grace worked for years as a cook in the railway service, then began preaching in the year 1925. "Grace" is an assumed name. Whether accidentally or by design, the name serves a useful purpose in the general pattern of his religious teachings. Today his churches dot the eastern seaboard in a score, or more, of strategic spots.

ORGANIZATION

The organization is fairly similar to that of Mt. Sinai Holy Church, but there are some marked differences.

Although Bishop Ida Robinson is actual head of Mt. Sinai by virtue of having been its founder, as well as by tradition, still she permits herself to be bound in some degree by the board of presbyters. Bishop Grace, on the other hand, is the undisputed head of the United House of Prayer. No board of presbyters appoints his preachers. He reserves this prerogative to himself. In private he is even known to boast that he will not have any preacher serve in the United House of Prayer whom he might consider smart enough to question his undisputed authority.

The task of the preachers is to carry out the instructions of the bishop, to conduct services and preach, and, perhaps most important of all, to raise money. All moneys must be strictly accounted for and returned to Bishop Grace through his Washington office. On one night a week the preacher is permitted to claim the moneys contributed for himself.

MEMBERSHIP

Theoretically membership is limited to those who have had a special experience, but actually the House of Prayer for All People, as its name implies, is open to anyone who desires to join. What special appeals induce members to come into the cult or to remain active after they have joined are indicated in the testimonies of various members which are included in Appendix A.

FINANCE

During each service there are numerous collections. Ushers who take up these collections in small aluminum pans vie with each other in their efforts to raise the largest amounts. They rush about the House of Prayer calling out, "Please put something in *my* pan!" "Please swell *my* total!" Some special honor or favor such as sitting on the right side of Daddy Grace when he comes to the local House of Prayer usually accrues to the person who collects the largest sum over a given period.

The definite money emphasis in this cult is indicated by the following extracts taken verbatim from the "General Council Laws of the United House of Prayer for All People":

6. There shall be no offering taken on the night that is set apart for Daddy Grace before his arrival to the mountain.

*   *   *

11. No pastor is to handle money. A sign shall be hung in each house of prayer to this effect.

     a. All pastors must teach the same. Any secretary or member giving the pastor money or other moneys shall he come short, he also shall be found guilty with the pastor that handled it.
     b. Each house must have a banking committee and a committee to pay bills unless there is a written order from Daddy Grace to do otherwise.

*   *   *

18. The House of Prayer in each state [of the United States] should insure all of their ministers and the balance over funeral expense not more than one hundred dollars should go to the House of Prayer treasurer as Beneficiary. This insurance policy must be taken with the Family Aid Association.

19. Ruled by the executive council each day and night during con-vocation where the Prophet is present there shall be an offering and a special sacrifice taken from the congregation for the extension of the gospel. This occasion must be boosted and made worth while occasion each night and day.

* * *

38. Pastors must be in knowledge of everything: every Penny raised and spent.

39. Each House must have representative a man besides the pastor to take note of everything and accompany the pastor at the time of checking.

40. All pastors must see to it that each member pays his convoca-tion fee and substantial rallies put on for the upbuilding of the King-dom of Heaven and this is to be put in the hands of our General Builder to build as he see fit without bounds.

* * *

48. All houses of prayer must raise money in a united drive to buy a car for our Daddy Grace.   Each state must do its part.

* * *

50. The state that wins the convocation victory will have an elab-orate banquet on the day appointed by Daddy Grace. [The convoca-tion victory is determined by the amount of money turned in.]   The convocation King, Prince, Queen, Princess and all of the honorable ministers, officers and members of the victory state will be the guests of Daddy Grace the Supreme.   The banquet will be given at the ex-pense of the loosing states.   Each loosing state will have to pay a cer-tain amount which will be named later.   Money left over the expenses of the banquet will be presented to Daddy Grace which he will do with as he desires.

As these extracts indicate, the members of the cult are divided into numerous clubs whose chief function is to raise money which will be turned over to Bishop Grace. Usually in the various houses of prayer there is a large poster on which lists of these clubs are shown with the amounts of money recently raised.

As a means of stirring social rivalry, but essentially for the pur-pose of increasing the totals which are to make up the collections for the leader, frequent contests are arranged, usually King and Queen contests, in which men and women attempt to win the honor of representing the local house of prayer on some special occasion.   Here, garbed in crêpe paper and tinsel, the victors will play the imperial rôles ordinarily associated with characters in fairy tales.

Instead of Mt. Sinai's one convocation a year Bishop Grace has arranged separate convocations in different states and localities. In each of these convocations sums of money are raised and turned over to the bishop. When all these district groups have met, a monster convocation is called in a selected place, and to this representatives from all over the East and South pour in. The scores of contributions from the local convocations are now augmented by one master contribution known as the national offering.[2]

SACRED TEXT

The sacred text is the Bible.

BELIEFS

In outward form and pretension the beliefs and practices are almost identical with those of Mt. Sinai Holy Church. That is to say, the cult represents a Christian sect of the holiness type, believing in conversion, sanctification, and the intervention of the Holy Spirit, etc. There are the usual taboos.

Actually, however, the beliefs boil down to a worship of Daddy Grace. God appears to be all but forgotten. The followers concentrate their thoughts on His "great man," Grace. Such a line of thinking is encouraged by Bishop Grace and by his preachers.

Thus Bishop Grace has been heard admonishing his worshippers:

Never mind about God. Salvation is by Grace only. . . . Grace has given God a vacation, and since God is on His vacation, don't worry Him. . . . If you sin against God, Grace can save you, but if you sin against Grace, God cannot save you.

Scriptural references by the dozens, in which the word "grace" appears, are quoted to demonstrate that "this man Grace" is the spirit of God walking among men.

The anthropomorphic quality of these beliefs may be readily discerned in a perusal of testimonial material included in this study.

---

2 The convocations are most spectacular. Usually there is a parade, in which Bishop Grace rides in state in a huge limousine, while dozens of his ministers walk afoot and take turns preaching to the multitudes who witness the parade from the sidewalks. In a recent convocation in Philadelphia a public baptism was performed, in which the neophytes presented themselves in bathing trunks near a fire plug, while the baptismal flow issued from a hose lent for the occasion by the local firehouse.

"Grace has given God a vacation..."
(BISHOP GRACE)

Crossing over Jordan

RITUAL

Typical Service

The service usually begins with unison singing, accompanied by piano or band. Then there is testimony. The singing is interlarded with shrieks, handclapping, stamping, and frequently concludes with the wholesale spectacle of a number of followers advancing to the front of the auditorium where they dance on the sawdust-covered floor. Other members flit about singly through the aisles and passageways. From time to time someone will collapse and fall prostrate to the floor. If the member is a woman, some attempt is made to prevent indecent exposure by covering her with a shawl or blanket. Oftentimes the leader, who may be an elder, a minister or simply a brother or sister will interrupt his speaking with a song in order to give the followers a chance to express themselves in a manner which obviously is very satisfying to them. All the while there is much calling out in tongues, which is said to be the Holy Spirit speaking through the human form but which actually appears to be a series of nonsense syllables. The preacher then reads from the Bible, interpolating remarks. He will call on an elder to assist with the reading, and after each clause read by the assistant he will call a halt, repeat the clause, and elucidate it. Usually the exposition is concerned with the spirit of "Grace" in the lives of the bishop's followers, or with the cardinal sins: fornication, adultery, lying, stealing, and backbiting. There is a frequent reference to the desirability of giving up everything, including all worldly possessions, to Daddy Grace. This extemporaneous preaching continues for varying lengths of time, depending on the hour of the day or on the particular financial need. At any point it is likely to be turned off abruptly and some pretext found for collecting an offering. The pastor may suddenly say, "Let us walk!" and, following him, the members will rise and walk to the altar on which a picture of Daddy Grace stands, genuflect before this, then raise the right hand and say a prayer, after which they drop money in a receptacle on the altar. (The altar is frequently referred to as "the mountain.") Such collections as well as the sale of magazines, and various commodities, interrupt the services, as do the songs and dancing. In another sense, of course, these are all part of the service. When the proper moment has arrived, the minister announces the next service, which will be later in the day or on the succeeding day, and the formal part of

the meeting is over.   By this time many of the followers already
have left the auditorium, or are otherwise engaged in various pursuits, such as selling the *Grace Magazine,* eating, or talking to
friends in the rear of the House of Prayer.

Another Typical Service

Approximately one hundred followers, chiefly women, are present at about 8:45 P.M.   One woman already lies prostrate on the
sawdust floor in the front of the temple.   Another woman is
dancing alone in a kind of dance indistinguishable from the latest
jitterbug form.   In the front of the auditorium is the picture of
Daddy Grace before which members genuflect and offer prayers.
The leader who stands in front calls for a song which is usually
in a minor key.   The bass drummer beats his drum and begins
to sing, aided by tambourines struck by women in various parts
of the room—one woman dressed in red and making grimaces and
queer gesticulations beats very weird rhythms.   Other men and
women clap their hands, while still others clap two pieces of
wood together.   There are cries of "Daddy!   You feel so good!"
"Sweet Daddy!" "Come to Daddy!" "Oh, Daddy!"   Then there
are brief testimonies, usually including references to cures of
headache, asthma, or indigestion.   More singing and dancing
follows.   Women become convulsed, contort themselves, cavort
through the house of prayer, finally falling in a heap on the sawdust.   They lie outstretched, inert.   If they show any sign of
life while lying there, some one rushes to cover their exposed
parts with a blanket or wrap.   Some of them rise and weep or
jump about excitedly, until they gradually grow calm and sit
down again.   The minister continues.   He extols Daddy Grace
soap, which he claims will reduce weight.   It has healing properties also, he states.   At that moment a very stout woman begins to dance up and down in her place.   The minister takes a
copy of the *Grace Magazine,* which sells for ten cents, and offers
it for sale.   "Put this magazine," he cries, "on your chest if you
have a cold or the tuberculosis, and you will be cured!"   He also
offers for sale Gospel stationery at two sheets and two envelopes
for five cents.   The stationery contains at the top the words "GOD
BLESS AMERICA," and beneath these the inscription: "The OK'ed
Faith of God, the House of Prayer for All People.   Isaiah 2:2;
Isaiah 56:7; Genesis 28:16–17."   More testimony and singing follows; more remarks and Bible references by the minister, more
singing, and then dismissal.

PRACTICES

The United House of Prayer for All People has meetings every night and all day Sunday.

The distinguishing characteristics of the practices of this cult are their extreme physical frenzy, and the use to which these frenzies are applied in raising money for carrying on their work.

Thus in one service I heard the preacher, who was expounding upon the duty of a wife to make sacrifices for her husband, turn off and remark, "And you see why you must give all you can for dear Daddy Grace."

Allusions to sex motives are numerous. In a moment of comparative tranquillity, I heard a preacher call out to the followers, who were chiefly women, "Who has the best thing you ever did see? I mean the best feeling thing you ever did feel? You feel it from your head to your feet. You don't know what I mean? Makes you feel good. Makes everybody feel good."

Such allusions, like the dancing, cause weird cries to emanate from various parts of the house of prayer. "Sweet Daddy!" "Oh, Daddy!" "Daddy, you feel so good!" "Daddy, Daddy, Daddy!" are typical expressions.

Followers are encouraged to dance ecstatically, but always with members of the same sex. Frequently the dancer falls to the floor and lies there many minutes. In order to break the fall, it is customary to cover the front part of the house of prayer with sawdust.

Throughout the meetings there is a constant succession of members falling on the floor. Sometimes scores of followers rush up to the front and participate in a sort of emotional marathon.

After a member has fallen and lain prostrate for a time, she is likely to arise suddenly, weeping profusely, and leap about, singing and dancing through the house of prayer. Gradually she becomes subdued, possibly she sits down on a chair or a bench, and eventually she resumes her normal manner. Soon thereafter she may be observed leaving the place, chatting and laughing with friends as if nothing had happened to her all evening.

If Bishop Grace himself is present, many worshippers will march or dance to the front and grasp his hand. Not infrequently the worshipper will place a bill of sizable denomination in his palm. Often the mere touch of the leader's hand is sufficient to induce terrific contortion of the body or to produce a state akin to catalepsy. The Bishop assured me there was nothing on his person (such as an electric charge) to account for this phenomenon.   He says it is the action of the Holy Spirit.

While these things are happening, time is taken to make collections, invite members to purchase food at the canteen, or to place on sale various Daddy Grace products which are an essential part of the spiritual exposition.   Thus Daddy Grace soap will cleanse the body, or reduce fat, or heal, according to the individual need.   Daddy Grace writing paper will aid the writer in composing a good letter.   Has the follower a cold or tuberculosis?   The *Grace Magazine* will, if placed on your chest, give a complete cure.

Similarly there is Daddy Grace tooth paste, transcontinental tea and coffee, men and women's hair pomade (which ostensibly cancels the taboo against beautifying the person), face powder, cold water soap, talcum powder, shoe polish, lemon cream, cold cream, pine soap, vanishing cream, castille and palmolive soap, and even Daddy Grace cookies.   There also is a home-buying association, and an insurance and burying society.

In addition there are numerous emblems, buttons, badges, banners, and finally elaborate uniforms with accessories of swords, batons, and walking sticks, whose sale swells the totals of funds employed by the bishop in his United House of Prayer for All People.

IV

CHURCH OF GOD (BLACK JEWS)

Mrs. I. is an intelligent woman about thirty-five years of age, married and the mother of two children. She joined Prophet Cherry's church about six years ago. She formerly was a member of a holiness church, but, according to her, their worship is a "tale," just a fake. The business of speaking in tongues is a joke. All the whooping and yelling, dancing, falling out and the like is indecent. She joined Prophet Cherry's church after her husband. She and her children observed the Passover all of last week. Every day they stayed in church from 9 A.M. to about 1 A.M. the following morning, and then went home to bed, after which they returned. Prophet is the source of all knowledge, a wonderful man. Pretty soon he is going to commence "sealing," which is to say, putting the visible seal on the forehead and the invisible seal in the heart. A person who has been sealed can skip around as he pleases; he hasn't got long to stay here and his fate is sealed. There are three heavens, one the earth on which we tread, the other in the air where the birds fly, the third far above the sun and stars. When we die the three parts of our body separate; the soul (blood) and the physical body go to hell. The spirit, which is the breath that comes out of the nostrils, goes back to God. Some day in the future there will be a resurrection. At the first resurrection the soul and the body will go up to heaven and meet the spirit. At the second resurrection (for the bad people) the spirit will meet its soul and body in hell. When there is a death of a friend or relative you must not visit anyone but the nearest friends of the deceased. You must not visit any outsiders. No one must look on the body except close relatives and perhaps some one appointed by the Prophet, else such people will be defiled by the dead. (Let the dead bury the dead.) The body must not be kept in the house, and it must not be sent to the temple. It must go immediately to the undertaking establishment.

Mrs. I. has been broken up ever since her baby girl died about three years ago, "from teething too hard." Then it was that she really learned to love her church; everyone cherished her, comforted her, and did things for her. The church is grand to its members. It looks after them and keeps them in food, clothing, shelter, and medicine.

[1] The language employed in this example closely follows that of the informant.

The Prophet is a rare man who knows everything and thinks of his flock constantly. He reads and speaks Hebrew, and has Hebrew taught to the children. Mrs. I. argued with a Jew over a Jewish star she was wearing on her dress. The Jew said that she had no right to it. She upheld her right, and finally she told him that even if he claimed to be white, his damned mammy was a black woman. Prophet Cherry does not allow any pictures of people; these will harm you, and besides the Bible says you must not make any graven image. Wine is good to drink, and you have to drink it in order to get its benefits. The Bible tells you to drink it. All kinds of food are forbidden in the Bible, especially the hog; just to touch the hog is to be defiled. You can find the Hebrew letters in the English Bible (the Psalm which has the Hebrew letters). The Prophet's church is much superior to the holiness and other churches because there you really learn something. None of the churches permit the members of the congregation to help read the Bible in the Scripture lesson, or to ask questions. Mrs. I. loves her Prophet so much that sometimes it is difficult for her to come home; she wants so much to be near him.

ORIGIN

The Church of God, known familiarly as the "Black Jews" or "Black Hebrews," was founded many years ago by Prophet F. S. Cherry. Prophet Cherry is an elderly dark brown man, with mixed gray hair, a prominent mole on his chin. Originally from the Deep South, which he refers to as a place worse than hell, or "a hell of a place"—the prophet believes God has given him an exclusive right to profanity—he has traveled to many of the far places of the world as a seaman, and all over the United States as a laborer and railway employe.

The prophet is conversant with Yiddish and Hebrew. On his pulpit he keeps both a Yiddish and a Hebrew Bible, to which he refers frequently. It is his claim that years ago, when he was far from his native land, the Lord approached him in a vision and touched him, thereby appointing him His prophet. Thereafter he was led back to America and to Philadelphia, where he was directed to establish the Church of God.

A completely self-educated man, Prophet Cherry boasts that he never spent a day of his life in school. Although he welcomes educated men to the services of the Church of God, usually assigning them places of honor on his pulpit, he frequently ridicules the educated, derides their manners and thoughts, and defies any of them to disprove a single one of his utterances. He is especially vituperative against the clergy, whom he lampoons in shocking fashion, calling them "damn fools," "wild beasts," "vultures," etc. Invariably he quotes Scripture to support these castigations.

Unlike the leaders in most of the cults studied here, who are distinguished in some manner by their dress, the prophet usually appears in the pulpit wearing a very ordinary blue coat, brown trousers, black shoes, and an old blue shirt minus cravat, with the collar buttoned and fastened by means of a clasp. Occasionally he will appear clad in a black academic gown, the sleeves striped with yellow. He also wears a golden bracelet on his right wrist and a conspicuous ring. Frequently he carries a staff. His authority for these additions to his dress are certain instructions in the Scriptures.

ORGANIZATION

Prophet Cherry is the head of the church. All matters must be referred to him, and he is the final arbiter. However, there are subordinate officers. The prophet appoints elders, who are his vicars. These may take his place in the pulpit, or may be sent to preach in distant places. He also appoints deacons, deaconesses, and secretaries, whose chief duties are to supervise the routine affairs of the church, to watch its finances, to assist in visiting the sick and similar functions. There is also a preaching class, made up of men and women who expound the gospel in the manner of the prophet. There are various clubs and social groups to look after the social life of the cult and to raise funds. The general atmosphere of the cult is like that of a close-knit club or fraternal order.

MEMBERSHIP

Membership is open to any "black" person desirous of joining. While it is preferable that the neophyte shall have had an experience, such as a vision or dream (spirit possession), this is not a prerequisite. Speaking in tongues, a common criterion of holiness worship, is looked upon with disfavor. So also is an excess of emotion, although it is always proper to sing rhythmically and to dance within the bounds of decency.

FINANCE

No collections are taken during the services. There is a receptacle hanging on one of the doors where anyone entering the church may deposit a coin if he so desires, but the running ex-

penses of the cult are met by the payment of tithes.   There are
also special fees for participation in certain services like the Passover.

One might state that the sacred text of the Church of God is
the Christian Bible, but it would be more correct to say that it
is the Talmud.   The prophet always refers to the Hebrew Bible
as his ultimate source.   Many of his followers study Hebrew in
the Monday night class conducted by the cult, and it is not un-
common to hear members quote directly from the Hebrew (although it is a question whether they know what they are quoting).

The followers of Prophet Cherry believe that they are the Jews
mentioned in the Bible.   They refer to themselves as *the* Jews or
the Black Jews.   They claim that the so-called Jew is an inter-
loper and a fraud.

The Black Jews believe in Jesus Christ, but they also believe
that he was a black man.   This is the basis of the prophet's offer
of $1500 to anyone who can produce an authentic likeness of
Jesus Christ.   Since all such pictures depict Jesus as a member
of the white race, these likenesses, according to Prophet Cherry,
are absurd.   The prophet's attitude towards this question is frequently conveyed to his followers by acts like the following: He
will pull out a so-called picture of Jesus suddenly and scream to
his followers, "Who in hell is this?   Nobody knows!   They say
it is Jesus.   That's a damned lie!"

The Black Jews believe it is wrong to call their place of worship a synagogue.   This name belongs to the edifices of the
white Jews.   They quote Revelations 3:9 to support their belief: "Behold I will make them of the synagogue of Satan, which
say they are Jews, and are not, but do lie. . . ."

Black people are the original inhabitants of the earth.   A proof
of this is contained in such a passage as Genesis 49:12.   Here we
are told about "red eyes."   This must refer to a black man, because a white man's eyes do not get red [allusion not clear].   The
first white man was Gehazi, who received his white color as the
result of a curse which was placed upon him for sin (II Kings
5:27).

God is black (Jeremiah 8:21).

Esau was the first red man (Genesis 25:25).

Jacob was a black man.

The so-called Jews are imposters, but God knows who are and who are not Jews (Revelations 2:9; 3:9).

April, and not January, is the first month of the year (dated from Passover).

There was prejudice against the black man far back in history. In Numbers 12:1, Moses is reviled for marrying an Ethiopian woman.

The members of the Moorish Science Temple of America (Moors) prove their unworthiness by the lineage they claim. Their contention that they spring from the ancient Moabites is something of which they should be ashamed rather than boastful about (Genesis 19:30–37).

The black Jesus came not to nullify the Old Testament, but to fulfill it.

There are three heavens, one on the earth, another up in the trees, and a third in the skies.

God made the world approximately six thousand years ago. Every two thousand years there is a great dispensation. Four thousand years ago there was the Flood; two thousand years ago Jesus came. At the end of the present century Jesus will come again and usher in the millennium.

Each thousand years of the earth's existence represents one day of the week. The seventh day, or Sabbath, which will usher in the millennium, will arrive A.D. 2000.

The Christian Saturday, and not Sunday, is the true Sabbath.

Black people sprang from Jacob, a black man. They should be called Israelites, which was Jacob's name after he had wrestled with the angel.

The fate of the black man, his slavery, and his ultimate deliverance are all foretold in Bible passages. (Jeremiah 12:9, Lamentations 4:8, Deuteronomy 28:15, 40, 41.)

After Gehazi became white, he still mixed with black folk. That is how the yellow race came into existence.

The Lord expects his followers to drink intoxicating liquors (Deuteronomy 15:26).

Preachers are dumb dogs (Isaiah 56:10).

Gentiles constantly harp that black folk like to steal. This is because they are still angry at Jacob, the father of black folk, for stealing Esau's birthright.

The world will not get right until the Black Jews go into high places.

All thought is manufactured in the heart.   The breath catches this and goes back to God and makes intercession there.

Speaking in tongues is nonsense.

Typical Service

Because of the distinctive character of this quasi-holiness worship, a description of the general surroundings is of interest. The church itself, located at 2132 Nicholas Street in North Philadelphia, has been remodeled from two adjoining houses, the second floor of which has been made into an auditorium.   To reach it there is a steep flight of very narrow stairs at the top of which is a room seating about three hundred people.

In the winter the room smells of both coal and oil, the coal fumes issuing from stoves used to heat the place, and the smell of oil from lamps of various shapes and sizes which give the auditorium the character of a Jewish temple.   These lamps are said to have come from the Holy Land.

Hebrew characters, written across the walls and on various signs, testify to the "Jewish" basis of the worshipper's belief. The male members of the church wear black skullcaps, which they remove or cover with a hat when they go out on the street. Many of the women are garbed in blue and white capes, with red and blue straw hats fringed with short tassels.

To the left and at the front of the room there is an orchestra, consisting of tambourines, drums, castanets, rattles, and guitars. There is no piano, which is unusual for such musical groups. Neither is there a choir, as such, but from time to time three or four young men known as gospel singers will come forward and entertain the congregation with improvised songs.   Throughout the congregation also there are tambourines and castanets, and these are added to the performance of the players.

Here and there throughout the auditorium are men who wear uniforms which resemble military dress, and from whose sides swords dangle.   Swords are hung from the walls also.

On an evening of service the members begin assembling about 8 P.M.   They open the service with singing, accompanied by the orchestra.   From time to time members rise and testify to the wisdom of the prophet and the mercies of the heavenly Father.

When the prophet arrives he mounts the platform and sits down behind a rather large lectern.   He participates in the

musical activities by beating a huge drum. Then he makes a
signal with the drumstick to indicate that the services proper
are about to begin. He gives six successive beats on his drum,
then pauses. He adds another beat, and calls for the singing of
a hymn like "Joy to the World," which he lines.[2] When the song
has ended he gives another beat on his drum, the congregation
rises and faces east. The members raise their right hands and
repeat a brief prayer in unison. While the congregation is still
standing another hymn is sung, such as "We Are Climbing
Jacob's Ladder." Then the congregation is seated. Prophet
Cherry reads a chapter of the Bible in English. He explains
the verses as he goes on, interrupting his remarks with personal
experiences and droll sayings. He calls upon different members
of the congregation to assist him in reading the verses. All members are encouraged to rise and ask questions or to make comments on the verses read or on the prophet's remarks.

The last verse is read in unison, the prophet first reading a few
words alone, then pausing, after which the congregation repeats
them, and so on until the entire verse has been read by leader
and congregation and the chapter has been finished. Next a
song is sung, once more to the accompaniment of the orchestra
and the prophet's drum. Then the prophet speaks. He casti-
gates preachers, calls them "dumb dogs," asserts that one policeman is worth twenty-five preachers because a policeman will
give up his life to save you or your property, but preachers want
to keep everything good from you, your money, your women,
your wine. He flays the white Jews for denying Jesus, and re-
viles all people who eat pork. He assures his flock that they,
not the white Jews, are the true Israelites. He bewails the fact
that the Gentiles (whites) have taken from the black folk their
land, their money, their names, and cursed them with the title
"Negro." He warns the whites that the world will not get right
until the black Hebrews go into high places. He will prove that
black folk are not Negroes, coons, niggers, or shines, and he calls
out to "all 'niggers' to get the hell out of the place!" He traces
the genealogy of black folk, going back to Noah, Shem, Japheth,
Ham, Lot, Abraham, Isaac and Jacob. He rails at the Gentiles
who "have not left you a spoonful of dirt for yourselves, have
taken your name, your religion and your government." Yet he
preaches love for all mankind, asserting that he could not be a

2 This refers to the manner of calling out the song to be sung line by line, the
congregation singing only after each line is called out by the leader.

child of God if he did not love everybody. He makes fun of a picture of Jesus, embarrassing a Baptist preacher who is seated on the rostrum by making him get the picture from behind his chair and hold it up to the congregation while he calls out, "I'll give anybody one thousand dollars tomorrow night who can tell me who the hell that is!" Thus he goes on for an hour or more. Near the end of his sermon he is likely to refer to the absence of collections in his temple, so unlike most Christian churches. "I'll kick the tambourine to hell out of here," he shouts, "if anybody tries to collect money on it!" Suddenly he calls for a song. The congregation rises. The prophet beats his drum. After the song the congregation again faces east, repeats the same words used at the beginning of the service, and is dismissed.

Purification Service

This service is held just before Passover. About 8:30 P.M. the prophet sits on the rostrum beating his drum while the congregation sings. This goes on until nearly nine o'clock. Then the prophet calls out a list of names. These are the members to be purified this night. The ritual of purification is as follows:

Beginning with the men, the prophet or his secretary reads out a name and the member rises and approaches the prophet, who stands at a washbowl placed in front of the pulpit. The prophet takes a clean towel and throws it over his shoulder. He tosses some perfume into the washbowl. The member washes his face and hands, and the prophet dries him with the towel. Member after member is called up, and this goes on for nearly two hours. The monotony is relieved somewhat by the constant singing of the members, assisted by the orchestra.

After this part of the ceremony is ended, the prophet walks up and down and around the room tossing perfumed water all about in order to purify the temple. One of the elders, a preacher, rises and mounts the rostrum. He testifies that only Prophet Cherry's children are the real children of God, and part of the proof of this is that they call their temple a "house of prayer" according to the biblical injunction, and not a synagogue as the white Jews do. Besides, he adds, they are the only group who are wise enough to recognize that April is the first month of the year. The Christians foolishly and sacrilegiously observe January as the first month of the year. Although it is nearing midnight the prophet now begins a long sermon, similar to his usual type of sermon as recorded above. Once more he rails against preachers, exclaiming, "I wouldn't give a damned preacher the smell off a dime!" He deprecates the numerous store-front churches among Negroes, and praises Jesus as the savior of men, but admonishes his followers to remember that Jesus was a black man with black forebears. He rails against the Pope, especially for condoning the rape of Ethiopia, and predicts that Hitler will drive him out of Rome. Referring to Jesus' birth, he points out the lie in the story that wise men came to see Jesus. Since Jesus was a black baby, Herod would have known that he was in Jerusalem had he remained there among all those white folk. But Jesus had been taken right off to Egypt, because there he was among people of his own color where his presence would not be conspicuous. Finally he reassures his followers, claiming that the Gentiles must rule the world for a spell longer. It is not in God's plan for the present that the black people shall uproot the Gentiles. Neither can Germany defeat America, because God has ordained that America shall be the last stronghold of the Gentiles. And as a final fillip he cries out, "Don't worry about Hitler coming to America! If he comes to America, he'd better not let anybody know he's here!" A song is sung, with orchestra playing and Prophet Cherry beating on his bass drum. The congregation turns to the east, repeats the usual incantation, and is dismissed.

PRACTICES

Services are held on Sunday, Wednesday, and Friday evenings, and all day Saturday, which is the Sabbath or Holy Day. The Sabbath begins at sundown Friday night and lasts until sundown Saturday.

Black Jews observe baptism, but the Passover is substituted for Holy Communion. They do not observe either Christmas or Easter.

Members call each other brothers and sisters.

There is little individual praying, but occasionally there is communal praying in which everyone gets down on his knees and makes his own prayer aloud simultaneously with others.

The Ten Commandments must be observed strictly. The prophet will read out of the church any person who is guilty of the more serious offenses.

Secular dancing is forbidden.

Drunkenness is forbidden, but moderate indulgence in intoxicating liquors is encouraged. The usual holiness sins, fornication, adultery, backbiting, etc., are very much taboo.

Black Jews must not eat pork.

Members must not have photographs made of themselves, or have pictures on the wall.   This is a violation of one of the Commandments.

When bathing in a tub, one should first wash the upper part of the body before entering the tub.   The water is bound to be defiled by the lower extremities.

Marriage outside the cult is not permitted unless the outsider agrees to come into the group.

The marriage ceremony is conducted in a manner very similar to the Christian.   The guests arrive fairly early at the home or church.   When everything is ready, a band of musicians plays a wedding march, and the couple approaches the altar and the marriage ceremony takes place in the conventional manner.   If the wedding occurs in the home, refreshments, including very strong intoxicants, are usually served.   It is considered improper not to partake of the liquid refreshment.

Divorce is not permitted, not even for adultery.   (An exception may be made if the innocent party actually finds his spouse in the act of adultery.)

Funerals take place in funeral parlors.   The deceased must be taken from the house as quickly as possible.   No one should see the body of the deceased save perhaps the very close relatives.

V

MOORISH SCIENCE TEMPLE OF AMERICA

TESTIMONY OF H. R.[1]

H. R. WAS born in Louisiana. From the age of seven years he could not believe in Christianity. At a church meeting one day he saw his mother fall out. All about her they said, "Loosen her corset!" He thought she was dying. But she recovered all right. A year or so later he asked her, "What was the matter?" She said she was just happy, that's all. He hated all that foolishness. Worst of all he hated the hypocrisy of the Christians. He wanted to be with his own and he never was satisfied until he became a Moslem. Then he learned there was no Negro, black or colored, and he's been happy ever since.

ORIGIN

This cult was founded about 1913 by Timothy Drew, who came from North Carolina where he was born in 1886.[2] Somewhere in his life he came upon two facts which radically influenced his thinking:

He encountered some forms of oriental philosophy and was impressed with its racial catholicity. The fruits of his research have been compressed into the *Holy Koran* of the Moorish Holy Temple of Science, which is not to be confused with the orthodox Mohammedan Koran.

He became obsessed with the idea that salvation for the Negro people lay in the discovery by them of their national origin, i. e., they must know whence they came, and refuse longer to be called Negroes, black folk, colored people, or Ethiopians. They must henceforth call themselves Asiatics, to use the generic term, or, more specifically, Moors or Moorish Americans.

Drew would harangue small groups of Negroes on street cor-

---

[1] See also Appendix A.

[2] In addition to information received from members and ex-members of the Moorish Science Temple of America, I am indebted to Arna Bontemps, noted author and historian, who made it possible for me to consult the files of the WPA Negro History Division in Chicago, where an historical study of this cult has been made.

ners, in basements, or empty lots. Although he had little formal education, a certain magnetic charm, a sincerity of purpose, and a real determination to lead his people out of the difficulties of racial prejudice and discrimination brought him followers.

He established his first temple in Newark, New Jersey. Gradually, as his following increased, temples were established in Pittsburgh, Detroit, and in numerous cities in the South. His greatest achievement was the founding of a temple in Chicago. But this was to prove his personal undoing.

Many Negroes on the South Side of Chicago flocked to the new teacher. Complete emancipation through a change of status from "Negro" to "Asiatic" promised an easy way to salvation.

When the initiate became a full member of the cult, he was given a card, slightly larger than a calling card, which bore the following inscription:

UNITY

(Replica of star and crescent)	(Replica of clasped hands)	(Replica of circled "7")
ISLAM		ALLAH

This is your Nationality and Identification Card for the Moorish Science Temple of America, and Birthrights for the Moorish Americans, etc., we honor all the Divine Prophets, Jesus, Mohammed, Buddha and Confucius. May the blessings of the God of our Father Allah, be upon you that carry this card. I do hereby declare that you are a Moslem under the Divine Laws of the Holy Koran of Mecca, Love, Truth Peace Freedom and Justice. "I AM A CITIZEN OF THE U. S. A."

NOBLE DREW ALI, THE PROPHET, 3603 INDIANA AVE., CHICAGO, ILL.

The hundreds of Chicago Negroes who carried these cards believed that the mere sight of the card would be sufficient to restrain a white man who was bent on disturbing or harming its holder.

The members were also taught to believe that a sign, a star within a crescent moon, had been seen in the heavens, and that this betokened the arrival of the day of the Asiatics, and the destruction of the Europeans (whites).

A number of disturbances developed. The Moors, made conspicuous by their fezzes, walked the streets, treating white folk with open contempt. In various parts of the Middle West they became anathema to the police.[3]

In Chicago, affairs reached the point where members of the cult would accost white people on the streets and, showing their membership cards or the button they wore in their coat lapels, would sing the praises of their prophet, now known as Noble Drew Ali, because he had freed them from the curse of European (white) domination. The prophet was compelled to call a halt to their zeal with the following admonition:

I hereby warn all Moors that they must cease from all radical or agitating speeches while on their jobs, or in their homes, or on the streets. Stop flashing your cards before Europeans as this only causes confusion. We did not come to cause confusion; our work is to uplift the nation.[4]

Climaxing these public difficulties, came troubles within the cult itself. Recognizing the need of assistance to extend his work, Noble Drew Ali took into his confidence some Negroes whose prior education fitted them to lead. Unfortunately they proved to have questionable motives, and before long had introduced practices which the prophet had not anticipated. Various methods were employed to exploit the members of the cult, including the sale of herbs, magical charms and potions, and literature pertaining to the cult. Some of the leaders of the cult grew rich.

When it became apparent that Noble Drew Ali stood in the way of further expansion along these lines, attempts were made to displace him. The internal strife reached menacing proportions, and eventually one of the leaders was killed. Noble Drew Ali who was not in Chicago at the time of the slaying, nevertheless, was arrested on his return to the city. He was remanded to prison to await trial for the death of the victim.[5]

[3] The profound character of this antagonism was impressed upon the author when he interviewed a member of the central police headquarters in Detroit about the activities of the Moors in that city. He became choleric with anger. "Those fellows!" he cried out. "What a terrible gang! Thieves and cutthroats! Wouldn't answer anything. Wouldn't sit down when you told them. Wouldn't stand up when you told them. Pretending they didn't understand you, that they were Moors from Morocco. They never saw Morocco! Those Moors never saw anything before they came to Detroit except Florida and Alabama!"

[4] See p. 11, note 22.

[5] During his incarceration he wrote his followers in this manner: "To the Heads of All Temples, Islam: I your prophet do hereby and now write you a letter as a warning and appeal to your good judgment for the present and the future. Though I am now in custody for you and the cause, it is all right and is well for

The trial never took place, for Noble Drew Ali, who had been released on bond, died a few weeks later, under mysterious circumstances. Some say he died from the effects of a third degree; others declare that his death was the result of a severe beating at the hands of dissident members.

Nevertheless he had lived long enough to imprint his life and reflections on the minds of his followers. Since his death they have split into numerous sects. Some claim to follow the spirit of the dead Noble Drew Ali, while others go so far as to believe that they now follow the reincarnation of Noble Drew Ali, that is, that their present leader rightfully claims to be the former prophet returned to the earth in another body. The Philadelphia temple which furnishes the chief data for this study holds to this belief.

ORGANIZATION

Because of the secret character of this cult, full details of its present organization are lacking. This much has been divulged to the author: The prophet (reincarnated) is the final authority. Nothing whatever can be done in any of the branches without his prior knowledge and assent; any command or instruction from him must be obeyed summarily. The leader of each branch temple is known as Grand Sheik or Governor. There are elders and stewards. Ordinary members are known as brothers and sisters (as for that matter the grand sheik is also). Every member is required to attach the term "el" (pronounced "eel") or "bey" to his name. The term "bey" appears to have a somewhat more distinguished connotation than "el." The insistence upon the addition of these titles has involved members of the cult in numerous legal disputes.

MEMBERSHIP

Membership is open to all "Asiatics." By Asiatic is meant any person not of "pale" hue (i.e., non-Caucasian). However, the author has not seen any Moors who were not Negroes.

Affirmation of a desire to be included on the rolls of the cult is the only prerequisite to admission. There is an initiation fee of $1.00, with certain stipulated dues thereafter.

all who still believe in me and my father, God. I have redeemed all of you and you shall be saved, all of you, even with me. I go to bat Monday, May 20, before the Grand Jury. If you are with me, be there. Remember my laws and love one another. Prefer not a stranger to your brother. Love and truth and my peace I leave you all. Peace from your Prophet, Noble Drew Ali."

FINANCE

Financial support is derived from two main sources: collections during the services of the temple, and dues.   Members frequently pay dues while they are attending the regular services of the temple.

SACRED TEXT

The various sects of the Moorish Science Temple of America live in accordance with the teachings divulged to and by Noble Drew Ali, as contained in the *Holy Koran* of the Moorish Holy Temple of Science.   This book is secret.[6]   There is also a catechism or questionary derived from the *Holy Koran,* which I was permitted to see.

The *Holy Koran* consists of 64 pages, rather compactly printed. The cover page reads as follows:

THE HOLY KORAN

of the

MOORISH   HOLY   TEMPLE
OF   SCIENCE

7

Divinely   Prepared   by   the   Noble   Prophet

DREW   ALI

BY the guiding of his father God, Allah; the great God of
the universe.   To redeem man from his sinful and
fallen stage of humanity back to the highest plane
of life with his father, God, Allah.

On the inside cover are the words:

KNOW THYSELF AND ALLAH
THE GENEOLOGY
OF 'JESUS'

Life and Works of Jesus in India
Europe and Africa, in the
land of Egypt.

---

[6] I strove for two years to look inside a copy of the *Holy Koran*.   I was not successful until I met an ex-member in Chicago who showed me some pages in his possession.   Shortly thereafter a young woman in Philadelphia obtained a copy for overnight perusal from a lax member who hoped to include her within the fold.   I was thus able to read the missing pages.   For the sake of interest I am sorely tempted to include extracts from this document in this study, but the Moors esteem their *Koran* so highly, that I fear to do so would be interpreted by them as a breach of trust.

The first page of the *Holy Koran* contains a picture of Noble Drew Ali. We see a tall, slender, dark Negro, with rather pronounced qualities of the dreamer suggested in his physiognomy. He is clad in dark trousers, dark shoes, a white robe and sash, collar and necktie, and fez.[7] His right hand, which is distinguished by long, slender, sentient fingers, is stretched across his breast. Under the picture is the sub-title:

THE PROPHET AND FOUNDER OF THE MOORISH SCIENCE
TEMPLE OF AMERICA, TO REDEEM THE PEOPLE
FROM THEIR SINFUL WAYS.

On the second page is a portrait of a Mohammedan priest or sheik, with title:

SULTAN ABDUL AZIZ IBU SUAD
THE DESCENDANT OF HAGAR, NOW THE HEAD OF THE
HOLY CITY OF MECCA

Then follows an introductory page of instructions.

The introductory page of instructions indicates clearly certain outlines in the beliefs of the Moors:

1. Although they are a Moslem sect, Jesus figures prominently.
2. The cult is secret.
3. Noble Drew Ali is a prophet ordained by Allah.
4. Allah is God, and He has ordained His prophet, Noble Drew Ali, to divulge His secrets to the dark folk of America.
5. Moslems (i. e., people of dark hue) belong to certain areas of the world including the American continent.
6. The guiding spirit of the universe is love.

After the introductory page, there follow many pages containing apocryphal chapters from the life of Jesus, and further pages of instruction, admonition, caution, warning, and reference to the rôle of the dark races in the world's development.

The concluding chapters, which are numbered 45–48, treat of the divine origin of Asiatic nations, the beginning of Christianity, Egypt as the capital empire of the dominion of Africa, and the End of Time and the fulfilling of the prophesies. In these chapters many of the racial principles of the cult are expounded.

On the inside of the back cover are these words:

[7] Since present-day Moors are characterized by beards and the absence of the necktie, it is to be inferred that these features of the cult have been added since the death of Noble Drew Ali.

The fallen sons and daughters of the Asiatic Nation of North America need to learn to love instead of hate; and to know of their higher self and lower self. This is the uniting of the Holy Koran of Mecca, for the teaching and instructing of all Moorish Americans, etc.

On the back cover occur the following words:

THE HOLY KORAN
of the
MOORISH SCIENCE TEMPLE
OF AMERICA
KNOW YOURSELF AND YOUR FATHER
GOD ALLAH
THAT YOU MAY LEARN TO LOVE INSTEAD OF HATE
EVERYMAN NEED TO WORSHIP UNDER HIS OWN
VINE AND FIG TREE
THE UNITY OF ASIA

BELIEFS

The charter of the Moorish Science Temple came from the great capital empire of Egypt.

Before you can have a God, you must have a nationality.

Noble Drew Ali gave his people a nation (Morocco).

There is no Negro, black, colored, or Ethiopian—only "Asiatic" or Moorish-American.

Ethiopian signifies a division.

Negro (black) signifies death.

"Colored" signifies something that is painted.

For the above reasons, the term Moorish-American must be used, and not other, opprobrious terms.

The name means everything; by taking the Asiatic's name from him, and calling him Negro, black, colored, or Ethiopian, the European stripped the Moor of his power, his authority, his God, and every other worth-while possession.

Christianity is for the European (paleface); [8] Moslemism is for the Asiatic (olive-skinned). When each group has its own peculiar religion, there will be peace on earth.

Noble Drew Ali is a kindred personage and spirit to Confucius, Jesus, Buddha, and Zoroaster.

---

[8] But "Jesus himself was of the true blood of the ancient Canaanites and Moabites and the inhabitants of Africa." *Holy Koran* of Noble Drew Ali, Chapter XLVI.

Marcus Garvey was to Noble Drew Ali as John the Baptist was to Christ.[9]

Typical Service

At 8 P.M. promptly, the leader, who sits at the front of the temple facing the congregation, begins to chant a hymn softly, and this is taken up by the members of the congregation. Unlike the singing in many Negro services, the chants of the Moors are very soft. Next the leader reads from the *Holy Koran* of Noble Drew Ali, and his voice is very low, scarcely above a whisper. When he has finished his reading, he makes a brief discourse to the members. He reminds them that they are the descendants of the Moabites and Canaanites, that they have a charter and that this charter was procured in the great capital in Egypt, and that it entitles the Moors to possession of northwest and southwest Africa. He emphasizes that Egypt is a greater capital than Washington. He reminds his followers that there is no Negro, black, colored, or Ethiopian, and that before they can have a God they must have a nationality. He proclaims the reincarnation of their Prophet, Noble Drew Ali, and states that he is in reality Mohammed III, who gave them a nation which he called Morocco. Christianity, he tells them, is the religion for the Europeans, but Islam is the religion for the Asiatics. When Europe and Asia each has its own religion, then there will be peace.

Christianity, he continues, is a European religion which was founded in Rome. The Romans killed Jesus, who was a Canaanite, and following the death of Jesus there was peace for a time. But Mohammed II came, and then there was no longer any peace. The name means everything, and by taking away the name of the Moors the palefaces stripped the power, authority, God, and everything from the darker peoples. Thus the Europeans have taken away their flag, their land, their God, their name—everything. The Moors must struggle on, establishing a world in which love, truth, peace, freedom, and justice will flourish. Always there must be peace, and although the Moors are hostile to the palefaces there must be no question of obedience to the American flag and loyalty to the United States.

9 Marcus Garvey was a Jamaican Negro who aroused a great wave of nationalism among Negroes in the United States and the West Indies immediately following the First World War.

After the leader has spoken, an elder reads the special laws of the temple which are in the questionary, and which also hang in a frame on the wall. This copy he takes down from the wall and reads. The elder makes comments as he goes along, similar to the remarks already made by the grand sheik. After he has concluded his reading, the leader again rises and picks up the *Holy Koran,* and invites members to come forward and speak. One after the other they approach the front, take the *Holy Koran* to testify. Each begins by saying, "I rise to give (do) honor to Allah, and to his Holy Prophet, Noble Drew Ali, Reincarnated, who gave to us this *Holy Koran."* Then follows reading from the *Koran* and a talk in the same vein as the one given by the leader. The individual talks will bear testimony to the efficacy of the spirit of Noble Drew Ali, Reincarnated, and how that spirit, or perhaps an actual word from the living prophet, has illuminated the life of the follower. Frequent reference is made to the fact that the prophet has removed the stigma of color and of race.

At 9:30 promptly, several members move forward with collection plates; the leader begins a chant, which is taken up quietly by the followers. Usually the chants are ordinary hymn tunes set to words which conform to Moslem teaching. For example:

"Give me that old time religion . . ."

becomes:

"Moslem's that old time religion . . ."

The collection takes about fifteen minutes, after which the followers continue to come forward, read from the *Koran* and testify until, exactly at 10 P.M., the leader gives a signal, everyone stands, faces east, raises the arms horizontally, with first and second fingers of the right hand uplifted, and says, "Allah, the Father of the Universe, the Father of Love, Truth, Peace, Freedom and Justice. Allah is my Protector, my Guide, and my Salvation by night and by day, through His Holy Prophet, Drew Ali. Amen."

Typical Sunday School Service

This service begins promptly at 5 P.M. and ends punctually at 7. The leader goes around the temple, starting from the front. He holds a questionary in his hand from which he asks questions in so low a tone of voice that it is impossible to hear him more than three or four feet away. Men and women assistants, some old, some quite young, also go about through the temple questioning in the same way. A remarkable stillness prevails. After the entire temple group, including the smallest children, have been given at least one question each, the leaders go again through the congregation and have the members, one by one, read one verse from an assigned chapter of the *Koran*. When this has been completed, the grand sheik reads the chapter aloud from the front of the temple, and calls for questions on the interpretation. When someone asks a question, the leader may clarify the text or he may call on others to give the proper answer. Later he calls for volunteers to repeat from memory a verse from this chapter. Then a brisk collection period ensues. It is nearly 7 P.M. Everyone rises, and repeats the religious formula given above. Now comes a respite until the 8 P.M. service.

PRACTICES

In connection with the services in the temple the following practices are especially to be noted, for they are quite distinct from practices to be observed at most Negro religious services.

When sitting in the temple, men and women are segregated. In Philadelphia it is customary to have the women seated in the front, the men to the rear.

All members are particular about having everyone pay strict attention to the service. Older members frequently are prodded because they nod during the service. But the pranks of the young children are regarded with an amazing patience and with an unusual degree of sympathy for the restlessness of children.

All services are extraordinarily quiet, belying the generally accepted beliefs regarding the Negro and his religious worship. Thus it often is extremely difficult to make out the words of a speaker addressing the congregation from the front of the temple despite the tomb-like stillness. Although there is some bustle as the women take care of the needs of their children, this is accomplished with a minimum of commotion or noise. Exclamations from the congregation are few and almost inaudible; there is a complete absence of that emotionalism which is considered characteristic of Negro services, and this is the more surprising because the basic principles of the cult involve those very elements which would be expected to arouse the emotions to an extreme degree. Finally, the meetings begin punctually and end punctually, a most unusual condition in Negro churches.[10]

10 On several occasions the grand sheik at 10 P.M. requested all "members" to remain a moment after service, which undoubtedly was a polite way of asking me,

The place of worship is not called a church; it is the temple.

Friday is the Sabbath of the cult.

"Christmas" is observed on January 5, the anniversary of the day when the prophet, Noble Drew Ali, was reincarnated.

Meetings of the cult are held Friday, Sunday, and Wednesday evenings. They begin at 8 P.M. and end at 10. There also is Sunday School from 5 P.M. to 7 on Sunday.

There is no baptism [11] or communion and little singing. There are few hymns, and these are mostly chants.

Members must pray three times daily, at sunrise, noon, and at sunset. When praying, members stand facing the east (Mecca), and raise their hands but do not prostrate themselves.

There are two words of greeting: "Peace!" and "Islam!" These are usually spoken with the right hand upraised, palm out.

All Moorish Americans must obey the laws of their (American) government. "Radicalism" is forbidden.

Marriages are monogamous. The grand sheik gives in marriage, and he may approve a union which would be forbidden under Christian auspices.

Divorce rarely is permitted.

Husbands must support their families. Wives must obey their husbands and care for their homes. Children must obey their parents.

Masters must be just to servants, and servants are to be patient under reproof.

Bodies must be kept clean by bathing.

The red fez should be worn by the men at all times, inside the house and temple as well as on the street.

Use of meat of any kind and eggs is forbidden. But fish and vegetables may be eaten.

Indulgence in European games, attendance at motion picture shows, and secular dancing are forbidden.

Shaving, cosmetics,[12] straightening the hair, use of intoxicants, and smoking are forbidden.

---

the only non-member, to leave promptly. No doubt, had I not been present, the business to be conducted in my absence would have taken place within the two hours normally allotted to the service.

[11] However, there is a reference in the *Holy Koran* which might be interpreted as symbolic baptism.

[12] An attractive young girl, a member of this cult, is known to employ cosmetics at her place of employment, but she is careful to destroy every trace before she leaves the place and goes out on the street to her home.

VI

FATHER DIVINE PEACE MISSION MOVEMENT

SING HAPPY is a tall, dark-brown-skinned, well-preserved Negro of about seventy years of age, with short gray hair and good teeth. He has a very strong baritone voice which is well known among the followers of Father Divine who join in the singing at Rockland Palace. One day many years ago Sing Happy heard Father call out to him in his apartment, "Happy!" He had been busy doing some small chore when suddenly he heard the voice call out to him. For a moment he could not imagine what or who it was. He rushed to the stairway to see, but there was no one. Then it dawned on him—Father! Some of his brothers assured him also it was Father. Several years ago, when it became necessary for him to register in order to vote, he realized he would have to have two names. Father had called him Happy, his spiritual name, because that denoted his type. But what should be his first name? He was in a quandary. Then it came to him. He was always singing. Of course! Sing Happy! And that is how he got his name. Sing Happy had traveled all around on the railroad, especially in New York, Chicago, and Cincinnati.

He had been sick nearly all his life. To begin with, his mother, who had six children, was a very sick woman when she bore the last three, of which he was one. They were weakly and had scrofula. At nine years of age he became badly afflicted with rheumatism. At the age of sixteen he contracted gonorrhea from a prostitute in his first sexual experience, and from then on this and syphilis kept him in constant ill health and misery, with frequent operations for stricture and stomach ulcers, and great difficulty in urination and defecation. In one operation a hemorrhage occurred, and in another some of the intestinal tract was removed. His second wife secretly raised an insurance policy on him, so sure was she that he would die. But it was she who died in 1918 and he has not married since, although up to the time he came to Father Divine he was always finding some woman to live with from time to time.

Meantime he had joined a number of churches, chiefly Baptist, but they did him no good, for several reasons: there was too much money collection with nothing in return, and too much wickedness by the

---

[1] The language employed in this example closely follows that of the informant.

members and the clergy.   The preachers could only offer one a better world in the future, that is, heaven.

He read his Bible and learned that the good should have everlasting life, that Jesus prayed for the continued life of his anointed, and that He kept them from evil.   But all the preachers could do about it was to promise one a reward in heaven.   He couldn't understand it and it didn't satisfy him.

He was living with two fellows who went with two sisters who used to visit them each week.   The three of them lived together like a happy family.   They trusted each other completely.   Then they all separated and it was several years before he saw one of the sisters, but by this time she and her man had joined Father Divine at Sayville; so that even though they were married, they now lived separately and were brother and sister.

They spoke rapturously about Father Divine.   Sing Happy still trusted these people completely.   He had read some reports of the persecutions of Father Divine at Sayville, and he was impressed by what he read.   He told them, "Tell Father Divine I am coming to his services and become a follower."

He was quite sure Father Divine was not a man, just from what he had read and heard, especially since Father Divine gave food and no one could tell where it began and ended.   So he visited Father Divine in New York, and he joined.   He has not missed a night in seven years ____ ___ he has been somewhere where there is not a Father Di-___.

____ ___ py says Father Divine cures.   Many rich people have been ___ ___ Father Divine.   Frequently they get their cure although they are thousands of miles away.   The big Duesenburg car which he rides was given him by an elderly white woman from California who had to wear braces on her legs but was cured by Father Divine.

Sing Happy says that Father Divine raises the dead.   The doctors pronounce them corpses.   They even place sheets over their faces. They go away a short while and lo! when they return, the dead are resurrected and are up eating.

Thus Mrs. ———, the wife of attorney ———.   She died just a few weeks ago.   But she returned to Rockland Palace to testify.   She was white as a ghost and very weak, but she testified how the doctors pronounced her dead and Father Divine came to her in a dream and breathed life into her body.   She is up and about now.   Sing Happy was at her house only a few days ago fixing some upholstery and she was quite spry.

Sing Happy says that when Father Divine was taken to court a few months ago seven judges feigned illness to keep from hearing his case. They feared they might die as Judge Smith [2] did, or as the clerk of the registry on 115th Street. After Father Divine had got a verdict from the Supreme Court saying that his followers might be registered to vote under their new names, one big fat clerk on 115th Street refused to register them notwithstanding. Father Divine went up to him and, pointing his finger at him, said, "You must obey the law. You must register my people."

The clerk nonchalantly blew smoke rings and said, law or no law, he was not going to register people with names like those. This went on for a few minutes; then the clerk had to go upstairs. Within a half hour after his refusal to register the voters he had died of a heart attack.

Sing Happy says Father Divine takes care of everything. He gives his followers a place to sleep in all his cities. He feeds them and keeps them for less than five dollars a week. He gives them clothes. He has their clothes cleaned and pressed for them. He has caretakers for his larger extensions, but in his small extensions each person takes care of his own bed.

When you need a haircut it costs ten cents, a shave, five cents, a shoeshine, three cents, an ordinary meal, ten cents, a chicken dinner, fifteen cents.

Sing Happy says that Father Divine encourages you to work. He is glad to have you keep your own money and spend it as you see fit. It is a lie that he has you turn in your money to him. He arranges for your trips to various cities; you have your railway fare or your b̲ ̲ ̲ all paid; your hotel accommodations and food are provided

Sing Happy says the whites are more considerate of h̲ ̲ own. He is referring to intellectual Negroes. All the ̲ leges are constantly sending delegations to observe, but his ̲ only criticize and scoff.

Sing Happy says if anyone finds any money it is turned over to Father Divine; and then if no one claims it (it is advertised in the *New Day*), it is used to provide excursions for poor children.

Sing Happy says Father Divine encourages business. His followers are in all kinds of business.

Sing Happy says people are always trying to "frame" Father Divine, especially to get money. But he owns nothing. That is why he has to stay in New York City (court order).[3] He may leave for twenty-three hours and twenty-eight minutes, and of course if he wanted to he could leave for as long as he wished. But he came to fulfill the law, not to break it. Consequently he carries out the law and remains there where there is plenty to do.

Sing Happy says that to become a member you come to meetings and make yourself known. You get acquainted and the other brothers see you and have a chance to size you up. If you wish, you can try

[3] At the time of publication, a similar situation is responsible for the removal of Father Divine's headquarters from New York to Philadelphia.

a period of living with the brothers even without being a member, in order to see if you could like it and could accommodate yourself. Then if you like it and all goes well, you become a brother and live in an extension.

Sing Happy says every once in a while some scalawag gets in.   He usually leaves of his own accord because he is not permitted to swear, drink, smoke, or have women, and he must have clean living habits. But sometimes it is necessary to advise him to go.

Sing Happy says Father Divine rules everything.   In order to change your routine you must get Father Divine's permission.   This permission Sing Happy would like to get in order to go to Kingston, New York, where a rich family wants him to do some temporary work. He has asked Father Divine for permission and is waiting to hear from him.

Sing Happy says he has been in at least twelve hospitals in New York City alone.   But since seven years ago when he joined Father Divine he has not seen a doctor or taken one drop of medicine.   His blood is all right.   He has daily evacuation.   His urethra is all right. He is able to eat anything at any time.

ORIGIN

The true history of Father Divine before he emerged in Say- ville, Long Island, is as much a mystery today as it was in 19__ when certain residents of Long Island, interested in having incarcerated for invading their hitherto exclusive precincts wit his mission, attempted to reconstruct it in the courtroom.   As a result of the prosecution, Supreme Court Justice Lewis J. Smith sentenced Father Divine to one year in the Suffolk County Jail, Long Island, and a fine of $500.   Three days later Justice Smith died suddenly and unexpectedly.   In the eyes of the followers of Father Divine, this was speedy substantiation of their claims that Father Divine is God.

There seems to be general agreement that he was once known by the name of George Baker (though he himself denies this); that he was born and raised in the Deep South, probably on an island off the coast of South Carolina; that he always had a flair for so-called mysticism, which early in his career resulted in a sentence to a chain gang in Georgia.   It may have been this experience and others like it which conditioned his thinking so that in the movement which he heads there has been evolved a plan for a "righteous government" in which there will be equality for all mankind, with the abolition of such evils as lynching and Jim Crow practices.

It is believed that Father Divine came north by stages, settling for a time in Baltimore. There under the name of Major J. Devine he opened a mission, where he distributed alms to the needy.

The early part of the depression of the thirties found him in Sayville, Long Island, where he had opened a lodging house and employment bureau. From there he transferred the center of his activities to Manhattan.

The growth of the Father Divine Peace Mission Movement in New York City has been one of the phenomenal occurrences in the history of the Negro in the North.[4]   In the metropolis alone there are more than a score of extensions, as the branches of the movement are called. Services are held at one time or other in all of these, but it is in the larger ones, where there are public auditoriums, that the most important occurrences take place.

There are similar branches in other cities and states throughout the Union, chiefly in the North and West, and even in other parts of the world.

ORGANIZATION

In the Father Divine Peace Mission Movement, Father Divine is the organization.

There are no assistants, no assistant leaders, no directors, vice-presidents, vice-chairmen, or elders. Whatever directive is carried out, no matter where it may be, has been issued or is assumed to have been issued by Father Divine.

The reason for such an organizational situation is not far to seek. Father Divine is God. He is everywhere, knows everything, sees and hears all things. Even though he dwells in New York City or Philadelphia a decision made by a follower in California could not have materialized independently, but must have been the result of spirit wireless directly from Father Divine.

In order to perform all the tasks devolving upon him in the metropolis, Father Divine is surrounded by secretaries, most of them women, white or Negro, who write down every word he utters and transmit his wishes to his followers near and far throughout the world.

The question naturally arises how any consistent work is accomplished if there is no organizational responsibility. The fact

---

[4] Since the transfer of the main headquarters to Philadelphia a similar growth is noted in that city where, according to the Negro press, the Father Divine Peace Mission Movement is "fast becoming the largest group of property owners among Negroes in the city" (1943).

is there is tremendous organizational responsibility; it is so tremendous and so forceful that followers strain themselves in their efforts to keep attuned to the spirit of their leader, whether he is present or absent, in order that they may know whether or not they have heard his call.

How intimately the leader is involved in every activity of each member of the cult is symbolized by Father Divine's service at the banquet table, known as the Holy Communion.   Every dish on which food is placed passes at least once through his hands. When a platter of meat is to be sent around, Father Divine places the serving utensil upon the platter with his own hands.   He places the ladle in the tureen of soup; he cuts the first slice of cake, pours the first glass of water, introduces the serving spoon into each container of ice cream.   He is thus part of every activity of the feast.

While theoretically there are no subordinates, actually there are certain figures who are recognized as important or outstanding in the general pattern.   John Lamb, the very efficient and ubiquitous personal secretary of Father Divine, is one of these. Father Divine's wife, known as Mother Divine, is a ranking member.   In the various cities and the different extensions one is likely to find some member who assumes a leading rôle; this is usually with the knowledge and consent of Father Divine.[5]

Such leadership is not always achieved with the explicit consent of Father Divine, because although Father Divine is God and is supreme and all-wise, nevertheless a branch can begin without his direction.[6]   It frequently happens that the first intimation of a new branch extension to reach Father Divine arrives long after the extension has been established.   Even at such a late moment, however, the extension becomes a matter for his consideration and approval.   Father Divine may approve or disapprove of the organization; he may approve or disapprove of the immediate direction of the extension; he may approve or disapprove of the content and method of instruction or method of operation.   Unless the work meets with his unqualified endorsement, it bears no relation to him and he will repudiate it even though it bears his name; in fact he will emphasize his repudiation for the very reason that it does carry his name.

[5] In Philadelphia, at the main extension at Broad and Catherine streets, this figure is known as Job Patience.

[6] In the *New Day* catalogue of extensions throughout the world there is appended this note: PARTIAL LIST—Because of the unknown number of FATHER DIVINE connections.

Thus, for thousands of his followers, Father Divine is the immediate as well as final arbiter. He meets scores of them daily, in one of his offices in New York City or Philadelphia, but frequently too in outlying extensions where he makes it a point to hold court, as it were, hearing requests, complaints, and grievances.

While much of the routine work must be delegated to secretaries, Father Divine is not too busy or too important to give personal consideration to what might seem to others the most trivial matters, such as a request of a member to take a trip from Philadelphia to Trenton, or to purchase a new suit of clothes, or to change living accommodations. He visits extensions and makes suggestions and criticisms; he goes out to the farms of the Peace Mission, in the "Promised Land," [7] and consults with or advises those members who have become farmers; he enters a Peace Mission restaurant or shoeshine parlor, or dress shop, and assays its services in terms of his requirements.

The numbers of the followers in this movement have been estimated from a few thousands to several millions. Either figure probably is extreme. After speaking to scores of Divinites, listening to hundreds of them give public testimony, and noting the character of that testimony, the author is of the opinion that there is a considerable secret, one might say unconscious, following of Father Divine which probably exceeds the many thousands of public followers who might be assembled in a huge convocation. These are chiefly those persons who are influenced by the real followers of Father Divine, although they do not themselves come under his direct and immediate influence. Father Divine himself probably will never know of the actual existence of many of these secret followers, yet they come under the influence of the Father Divine Peace Mission Movement, and to a certain degree they are subject to the discipline of the leader, i.e., indirectly they fall into his organizational scheme. If this is true, the function of this movement on the socio-economic-political level becomes more significant.

MEMBERSHIP

It is not easy for an outsider to explain the rules of membership. Unlike the Moorish Science Temple, where membership is granted automatically to any "Asiatic" on the basis of his de-

[7] Name given to choice extensions located in the Hudson River Valley.

sire to be included within the cult and certain other minor considerations, there is no fixed rule for membership in the Father Divine Peace Mission Movement.   Nor could it even be said that the rather indefinite rules of membership which apply to Mt. Sinai Holy Church apply here.

Sing Happy, himself a member of the Father Divine Peace Mission Movement, has indicated in his quoted remarks, the way by which one becomes a member of an extension group.   He refers to a trial period followed by the acceptance or rejection of the applicant.   This trial period might be compared with those already referred to in such groups as Mt. Sinai, but obviously there are major differences, since membership in the Father Divine Movement is the result of judgments by persons who are the equals of the prospective member, and not by a committee of elders as in the other cult.   The only person who holds higher rank in the Father Divine Peace Mission Movement is Father Divine himself.

One fact which makes it difficult to speak with finality about membership in this group is that any person, whether a member or not, is admitted to practically every activity of the cult.   Thus, although I was not a member (in fact in some respects I was *persona non grata* because of Father Divine's aversion to writers), I entered an extension at Greenkill Farms outside of Kingston, New York, where I was cordially received and was allowed to partake of all the privileges of a member (and of course observed all rules which a member would be required to adhere to).   The only apparent difference in my treatment and that of members was that I was required to pay a fee of two dollars a week for lodging, and approximately fifteen cents a meal for my board.   Otherwise everything was absolutely free.

There appear to be two types of members.   A great many members merely subscribe to the beliefs and practices of the cult, but otherwise live their lives normally as citizens of their community.   These are commonly known as brothers and sisters.

The other type of member seems to have gone a step farther.   He has renounced the things of this world completely.   He no longer plans his own life, but lives it completely in accordance with the instructions of Father Divine.   If he is the possessor of worldly goods, he disposes of them in a manner agreed upon between him and the leader.   He does not choose his own vocation or business, but places himself at the disposition of the Father, making himself completely subject to Father Divine's suggestion, instruction, or command.   Literally everything which such a member receives, the bread he eats, the raiment he wears, his lodging and work, whatever personal remuneration he may receive, comes through the direction of Father Divine.   Such members are the true angels of the cult.

I must emphasize that these are judgments formed as the result of conversations with dozens of Divinites from many walks of life.   It does not answer completely the question of membership, which I believe can be answered only as a result of a rather long experience as a member in the cult.   Neither does it fully answer the question which is uppermost in the minds of many people who inquire about this movement: Where does Father Divine get the resources to carry on his work?   But it does indicate that the movement possesses a mechanism by which it can be self-supporting, yet on the score of democracy can give considerable freedom to persons who wish to be members but prefer to live outside the sphere of complete dependence on the cult.

FINANCE

I have indicated above that the question of finance in the Father Divine Peace Mission Movement is unanswerable at the present time.   No collections of any kind are ever taken at a Father Divine Peace Mission Movement service.   Undoubtedly huge sums of money are required to carry on the work of the movement, but I have no information in regard to the source of these funds.

SACRED TEXT

The sacred text of the Father Divine Peace Mission Movement is not the Bible, but the *New Day,* a weekly periodical issued by the organization.   Followers invariably refer to this book rather than to the Bible when they wish to speak with authority.

The only time I ever saw a Bible in a Peace Mission meeting was when Father Divine announced that he had had his secretaries bring in two huge Bibles in order that any visiting preachers who were in the audience might feel at home.   The remark produced laughter in the audience.[8]

Father Divine discourages reading the Bible, as statements of members included in this study will reveal.   Some members say

---

[8] This no longer is true.   On the lectern of the main auditorium in Philadelphia there now rests a huge Bible (1943).

Father Divine *is* the Bible, so why read it? Certain it is, the Bible of the Peace Mission Movement is the *New Day*. It is read at all meetings. It contains every speech uttered by Father Divine, and many other pertinent speeches and facts.

The *New Day* is the outcome of the *Spoken Word,* a periodical which appeared for the first time in 1934. Then it consisted of a few pages of printed matter, chiefly speeches by Father Divine, and a scattering of advertisements. The copy of the *New Day* which I have before me as I write contains 132 pages, many of them filled with the words and deeds of Father Divine, and with more than 350 advertisements, including some from such well-known commercial houses as F. W. Woolworth Company, Loft Candy Corporation, Fuller Brush Company, McCrory Five and Ten Cent Stores, Daniel Reeve Company, and Lerner Shops. Every advertisement includes somewhere within its text the injunction: "Peace!" Frequently there is added, "Thank you, Father!"

A few headings of speeches by Father Divine, and other data contained in copies of the *New Day* are enlightening in regard to the general nature of the content and the philosophy of the movement:

1. FATHER'S LOVE HAS CAUSED YOU TO DO THINGS THE GOVERNMENT TRIED TO GET YOU TO DO: STOP COMMITTING VICE AND CRIME AND SIN AND DEBAUCHERY OF EVERY KIND

2. IF YOU HAPPEN TO BE A LAW VIOLATOR, A LAWBREAKER, AND A PROFANE PERSON, MY SPIRIT, MY LOVE, AND MY MIND WILL GO OUT AND GET YOU

3. WHATEVER I DO AND WHATEVER I AM ALLOWING TO BE DONE, ENDORSEABLE, IT IS FOR THE BENEFIT AND BETTERMENT OF ALL OF YOU

The headings to three photostatic copies of letters by war industries to Negroes who had applied for work with these concerns are indicative of the cult's political orientation:

1. AMERICAN RED CROSS WRITES DOCTOR THAT ONLY W———— [9] CITIZENS ARE ELIGIBLE FOR THE DOCTORS-FOR-BRITAIN PROJECT

[9] Note the use of W---- for "white," C------ for "colored," and "so-and-so" for Negro. Father Divine forbids the use of terms denoting distinctions of color and race.

2. U. S. NAVY DEPT WRITES APPLICANT SEEKING ENLIST-
   MENT IN NAVAL COMMUNICATION RESERVE THAT
   C——————— PERSONS ARE TAKEN ONLY IN THE MESS
   ATTENDANTS BRANCH OF THE SERVICE

3. CURTISS WRIGHT TECHNICAL INSTITUTE INFORMS
   APPLICANT THE AIRCRAFT INDUSTRY WILL NOT EM-
   PLOY MEMBERS OF THE SO–AND–SO RACE

BELIEFS

We have seen how the Moors believe that Noble Drew Ali was
Allah's divinely-inspired prophet, and the present Noble Drew
Ali is the reincarnated form of the prophet; how her followers
believe Bishop Ida Robinson is ordained by God; how Prophet
Cherry received his mantle directly from God in a vision; how
Bishop Grace is the very "grace" of God about which the Scrip-
tures speak.

In the Father Divine Peace Mission Movement, Father Divine
is God.   This fact is accepted without question or cavil by his
followers.   They believe this emphatically and unequivocally.
There are no ifs, ands, or buts, and this is as much the case with
the most highly cultured follower as it is for one who was formerly an illiterate share-cropper.

What is to occur should anything happen to Father Divine is
an unintelligible question to any follower in the movement.
Nothing can happen to Father Divine.   He will never die; he
is God.

It is impossible, through the written word, to convey the full
import of this concept, just as it is impossible to describe the
impression which comes over an outsider who listens to a highly
intelligent, sophisticated, and cultured young follower averring
this fact with a degree of quiet assurance which defies the imagination.   The bare fact remains: For the followers of Father
Divine, he is God.

Father Divine has come in his present form because the Negro
is one of the lowliest of creatures on the earth.   God prefers to
bring salvation to the lowly.

There is an end of "prophets" of God.   There will be no more
prophets, because God has wearied of the way people on earth
have repudiated former prophets.   Therefore, in these latter
days, God has returned to the world in person.

Heaven is on earth.   Only a select few will be saved.

There is no more baptism with water.   Now that God has
come, baptism in his spirit is available to every believer.

"Holy Ghost, speak through me!"

"I have mastered the economic situation!"
(FATHER DIVINE)

The Holy Communion is to be celebrated around the banquet table. Instead of wine and bread, "the abundance of the fullness" should be enjoyed, that is, all varieties of food and non-intoxicating drinks are to be served.[10]

No follower should refer to the passage of time with reference to Father Divine, because that constitutes interference with him.

Dates and places of past events must be put out of mind, because they are associated with human living and take the mind off matters of the soul.

Preachers are suspect. Father Divine nevertheless criticizes no creed or cult.

The righteous man is the reincarnation of the expressions, versions, ideas, and opinions of God. The closer a man lives to true evangelism, the more nearly will he approach the appearance of God.

A true follower of Father Divine will never die. Death is the last weakness which the faithful are to overcome. If even those of great faith fail to conquer death, the spirit enters another body and continues thus to live.

Illness is a sign that you have strayed from the faith which Father Divine requires. Somewhere you have failed to live evangelically. If you continue in this way, you will die.

To receive all possible blessings from God, one must give up all.

In times of doubt and trouble, the faithful must think only of Father Divine. They must say, "Thank you, Father," and then

[10] Much sport has been made of the heavily laden banquet tables of the Father Divine Peace Mission Movement. The criticism is often made that people join the movement because there is so much to eat. The interesting thing about the case material in this study is that eating is hardly ever advanced as a reason for having come into the movement. The more likely reasons are discussed at some length in a subsequent section. There is a common opinion also that the guest is supposed to eat everything placed before him. This is no more so than it is that a person in a restaurant is supposed to eat everything on the menu. A Father Divine banquet offers a great variety of foods from which the guest is expected to select those dishes which appeal to him. The menus at the great communion feasts are tremendous in their variety. At one such dinner I noted the following dishes: ham, roast beef, lamb, roast chicken, fried chicken, sliced white meat of chicken, filling, fish, white rice, mashed potatoes, macaroni, beets, corn on the cob, greens, cabbage, string beans, cauliflower, carrots, coleslaw, bologna, tongue, another form of beets, corn bread, white bread, whole wheat bread, pumpernickel, raisin bread, rye bread, rolls, crackers, pineapple salad, sliced tomatoes and lettuce, platters of celery, pickles and relishes, jellies, various kinds of layer cakes, iced tea, iced coffee, chocolate, lemonade, cheese, fruit, fruit cup, nuts, jello with whipped cream, ice cream.

they will arrive at the solution of their difficulties.   Through belief in Father Divine, any good wish may be materialized.

To live evangelically, one must refrain from stealing, refusing
to pay just debts, indulging in liquor in any form, smoking, ob-
scene language, gambling, playing numbers, racial prejudice or
hate of any kind, greed, bigotry, selfishness, and lust after the
opposite sex.

It is not impossible for a woman to conceive and have a child,
but if she has been living evangelically, such conception will be
the result of a spiritual union.   In the absence of proof, it would
be assumed that the birth of a child was the result of a violation
of the evangelical code.

Typical Service

In the auditorium are a number of Negroes of both sexes, and
a sprinkling of whites.   The men and women usually are separated, although occasionally couples are seated together.   Some
of the members are on the platform in the front of the auditorium, and from time to time one of these arises, or a member
from the floor mounts the platform and begins to sing or to testify.   At this particular meeting there is no musical accompaniment, though usually there is a band of musicians including piano, drum, saxophone, and possibly a stringed instrument.   Job
Patience, a West Indian, is chairman of the meeting, and he rises
to address the group.   He refers to Father Divine's Righteous
Government.   He speaks of the fourteen planks in the Righteous
Government platform.   He points to the placards that adorn the
meeting place, which likewise are reminders of the Righteous
Government, and also to the placards which decry the action of
a certain judge who is accused of prejudice against Father Divine
in a recent issue which came up in the courts.   Now he is lean-
ing heavily on the lectern, on the front of which is engraved a
crown surmounted with the letters A D F D, meaning "Anno
Domini Father Divine."   The leader exhorts the followers to
come up and express themselves.   Various members respond, including prominent professional people or politicians.   These
speak generally of the good effect of Father Divine on the morals
and behavior of members of the community.   The testimony is
interrupted from time to time as an individual in the audience
breaks into song, which often leads to dancing.

Suddenly a woman enters the hall and whispers to someone. "Father is here!" is the message. A stir is noticeable throughout the place. More people are streaming in. Additional musicians, a clarinetist, cornetist, take up the song. A general, lively expectancy fills the place, with the horns and drums contributing their part to the excitement. There is a spontaneous burst of hand-clapping. People rise, wave handkerchiefs, and cheer. Father Divine is entering the room.

He is an extremely short man, certainly under five feet, and although presumably he has lived many years, his stride and manner are as vigorous and buoyant as a youth's. His clothes are perfectly tailored, displaying a subdued flashiness and bearing no semblance to the usual priestly garb. His dark brown head, nearly bald, is strong and round. A glance at his eyes reveals native shrewdness and a keen sense of humor, but should there be any reason for his returning the glance, they seem unusually keen and penetrating. His powerful body was intended for limbs considerably longer than those on which he moves jauntily up the aisle, making more emphatic the suggestion of great power of will, determination, and command written in the firmly modeled full lips and widespread nostrils.

He walks briskly forward, followed by a corps of secretaries, and selects a seat at the rear of the platform. There he remains for a time somewhat sequestered. Soon he joins in the singing, at the same time kicks his feet against the floor, swaying his body to and fro, and clapping his hands lustily. More testimony and more singing follow when suddenly Father Divine leaps up, strides to the lectern and says a brief word of greeting. He resumes his seat and the singing and testimonials continue.

A short while afterwards, Father Divine again rises and proceeds to speak. He announces he will not do much speaking "yet," but instead he will let the pictures do the talking. (It is a service which is to culminate in motion pictures.) There is much groaning throughout the hall because he is not going to speak at length. Soon the movies are shown. There is a children's picture, a picture of Roosevelt's third inaugural, one on the life of St. Paul, another depicting scenes from the life of Father Divine at one of his farms, and then an industrial film issued by one of the large corporations of the country. While the movies are being shown, Father Divine leaves the room, but it is rumored that he will return at midnight, when there will be a feast in the banquet hall.

PRACTICES

There are no food taboos.

Intoxicants are strictly forbidden.

Dancing with members of the opposite sex is strictly forbidden.

Speaking in tongues is tolerated but not essential.

Business enterprises are encouraged.

Any display of racial intolerance is strictly forbidden. Where white and Negro members live together, arrangements should be made so that they eat and sleep together and not separately.[11]

The terms "Negro," "white," "black," and "colored," are strictly forbidden. The term "other expression" is employed, also "so-and-so."

There is no marriage; consequently there can be no divorce.

In the case of married couples who enter the cult, divorce is unnecessary since man and wife automatically separate when they become brother and sister in the cult, thereafter to have no regard for any member of the opposite sex.

A true follower will forget all else save Father Divine and his teaching. If he has mother, father, sister, brother, wife, or children, he will forsake these, unless they choose to come with him and follow Father Divine. An exception is made for minor children. A parent must be concerned about the rearing of his children, irrespective of membership in the Peace Mission Movement.

A frequent question of the author's whenever he was near Father Divine's banquet table at Rockland Palace, New York City, was how the various followers seated around the table were selected, since there were thousands of additional followers seated outside in the main auditorium who presumably were not invited to the banquet table. The answer from members usually was, "If you are supposed to sit at the banquet table, you will receive a message from the Father. When that message is coming, you will know it. Then you will go to the table and a place will be ready for you."

11 Of all the cults observed in this study, the Father Divine Peace Mission Movement is most insistent about breaking down all barriers of race and color. It is said that no law is more rigidly enforced than the one which forbids any kind of racial discrimination. On this account it would appear that the Father Divine movement has little chance to spread in the South. It is true that most of its operations are at present confined to the North and West. Nevertheless, the laws regarding sex separation and sex purity are also so strict that it is conceivable that even in the South little objection would be found to the movement. In fact, it may be that the very strict sex taboos have been designed, in part, to overcome the southern objections to the growth of the movement should it ever make encroachments on that part of the country.

At one of the Sunday night communion services at Rockland Palace, Father Divine said, "Do not stray from my teachings. There was a member here who, for a price, was arranging for people to sit at my communion table. I warned that member, but she continued her evil practice. She got ill, and then they had to take her to the hospital. Not long after, she passed." In a movement where eternal existence is dependent upon living "evangelically" on this earth, the compulsion of such an admonition is not hard to understand.

The followers of Father Divine view him with the greatest awe and the most profound devotion, yet they feel very close to him, and are free to approach him with any question, opinion, or request. A frequent expression to be heard among his followers, male and female, is "He's so sweet!"

Should a follower have to wait unduly long before seeing Father Divine, or should he fail altogether to communicate with him, such is the internal discipline of the movement that the follower will not question the integrity of his leader, or even of some individual in the movement who may have stood in the way. Instead he will assume that the proper spirit of harmony with Father Divine has not been established. Consequently he will look within himself to find what is lacking to establish the contact.

The comings and goings of Father Divine are signals for the wildest demonstrations among the members. The writer was in Nazi Germany at the beginning of Adolph Hitler's rule, but he saw nothing in the enthusiasm and fanatical worship of Hitler's followers to surpass in intensity the enthusiasm and devotion of the followers of Father Divine.

VII

COMPARATIVE STUDY

THE following order probably represents the degree of conformity of the cults studied with the more orthodox evangelical Christian denominations:

> Mt. Sinai Holy Church
> United House of Prayer for All People
> Church of God (Black Jews)
> Father Divine Peace Mission
> Moorish Science Temple of America

Mt. Sinai and United House of Prayer

These two cults are considered together because in many respects they are similar, particularly with regard to their organizational forms and religious practices.

There is little substantial difference in fundamental belief between these two cults and the orthodox churches. Thus there is a belief in the Holy Trinity although, in the case of the United House of Prayer, Bishop Grace becomes almost a fourth figure. Baptism and the Holy Communion are observed; individual prayer is a part of the ritual, but communal praying is more customary. The millennial resurrection of all souls is preached. Christmas and Easter are the important religious holidays.

In other words, the chief difference between worship in these two cults and many of the orthodox evangelistic churches lies in the manner in which the end object, salvation, is achieved. This difference is greater in the form of service than it is in the concept itself.

Summary Evaluation of Mt. Sinai Holy Church

CONFORMITY WITH ORTHODOX EVANGELICAL PATTERN

Divine Phenomena:
  God, Jesus, Holy Ghost, (Devil)
Rites: Baptism; Holy Communion, (washing of feet)

Apocalyptic concept of life after death (Heaven and Hell)
Conversion (sanctification and unusual experience)
Sacred text: Bible

DEVIATIONS FROM ORTHODOX EVANGELICAL PATTERN

General Emphasis:
   Tongues and other evidences of possession
   Dancing (music)
Manner of praying
Testimonies during ordinary services
Insistence on sanctification and unusual experience
Importance of leader

Summary Evaluation of United House of Prayer for All People

CONFORMITY WITH ORTHODOX EVANGELICAL PATTERN

Divine Phenomena:
   God, Jesus, Holy Ghost, (Devil)
Rites: Baptism, Holy Communion
Apocalyptic concept of life after death (Heaven and Hell)
Conversion (sanctification and unusual experience)
Sacred text: Bible

DEVIATIONS FROM ORTHODOX EVANGELICAL PATTERN

Importance of leader (paramount)
General Emphasis:
   Tongues and other evidences of possession
   Dancing (music)
   Money raising
Manner of praying
Some segregation of sexes in place of worship
Testimonies during ordinary services

Church of God (Black Jews)

In some respects this cult might be called a Christian sect, but it seems to me proper to classify it as a modified Judaic form. The basic sacred text is the Talmud but, in the absence of a New Testament in Hebrew, the English New Testament is also used. However, not all the generally accepted Christian tenets are held. Thus the followers refuse to be known as Christians, but call themselves Jews or Black Jews (Hebrews). They do not celebrate Christmas or Easter, but their Passover and Purification rites are a kind of combined Christmas-Easter celebration. Instead of the Holy Communion, the Passover is observed. Baptism, which is a Christian rite, is included in their holy observances.

The Black Jews accord to Jesus an extremely high place in their consideration. The direction of their thinking becomes clouded at this point. At one time they give the impression of adhering to the Judaic monotheistic belief, but again they will speak of the Father, Son, and Holy Ghost. They have the apocalyptic concept of heaven, but instead of one heaven there are three. Since one of these is on the earth, presumably a man is in heaven while he lives, and goes to heaven after he dies. (See individual testimonies in Appendix A.)

The method of becoming one of the elect is very similar to that of Mt. Sinai or the United House of Prayer. Here too there is little or no individual praying. The music is much more spontaneous than in the ordinary evangelical church service, and there is restrained dancing. The giving of testimonies during the service distinguishes the form of this worship from most of the orthodox evangelical forms. There is great importance attached to the person of the leader, Prophet Cherry.

Summary Evaluation of Church of God (Black Jews)

CONFORMITY WITH ORTHODOX EVANGELICAL PATTERN

Divine Phenomena:
  God, Jesus, Holy Ghost, (Devil)
Rites: Baptism
Apocalyptic concept of life after death (Heaven and Hell)
Conversion (sanctification and unusual experience)
Sacred text: Bible

DEVIATIONS FROM ORTHODOX EVANGELICAL PATTERN

Importance of leader
Rites: Purification and Passover instead of Holy Communion
No observance of Christmas or Easter
Three heavens
Dancing (restrained), (music)
Headdress of men worn in temple
Rise and face east to pray
Testimonies during ordinary services
Some segregation of sexes in place of worship

Father Divine Peace Mission Movement

I have called this cult "Christian eclectic." It appears to have Christian elements, and at first glance one is taken in by these

appearances. Actually, however, except for the recognition given
Jesus with regard to his proper sequence in the general scheme
of divine unfoldment, a closer scrutiny of this cult reveals that it
departs radically from orthodox evangelical belief and practice.
Not only is Father Divine God, but as God he has modified
numerous practices and dogmas until in some respects a new religion has been created. There is no baptism, no washing of
feet, no christening of infants. The Holy Communion exists in
name, but is so completely different from the usual form or concept as to be another rite. The Bible is regarded with reverence,
but the *New Day* likewise becomes a sacred book for all members.
There is absolutely no praying, with the exception of the stereotyped expression, "Thank you, Father!" which one utters whenever one is prompted to pray. There is no life after death for
the true worshiper, because for him there is no death. Members
who fail to live up to the evangelical demands of the cult, and
die as a result, return to this life in another body, and attempt
once more to live evangelically. Heaven is on earth; yet there
is also an apocalyptic concept of heaven, as divulged in the testimony of members. There is tacit recognition of the Son and the
Holy Ghost (Father Divine is God). Conversion is essential,
sanctification if anything is still more essential, while possession
by the Holy Ghost is an experience which every true member
must have had at some time in his evangelical life.

Summary Evaluation of the Father Divine Peace Mission

CONFORMITY WITH ORTHODOX EVANGELICAL PATTERN

Divine Phenomena:
   God (?), Jesus, Holy Ghost
Rites: Holy Communion (?)
Sacred text: Bible (?)
Apocalyptic concept of heaven (?)
Conversion (sanctification and unusual experience)

DEVIATIONS FROM ORTHODOX EVANGELICAL PATTERN

Father Divine is God.
Rites: No baptism. Holy Communion completely different from
   orthodox form
No concept of life after death, but a constant effort to achieve eternal
   life on this earth
Heaven is on earth.
"Thank you, Father!" is the only prayer
Excited dancing (music)

Tongues (?)
Segregation of sexes in place of worship and wherever possible
Testimonies during ordinary services
Sacred text: *New Day* (Bible?)

Moorish Science Temple of America

The Moorish Science Temple of America explicitly expresses its variance with Christian dogma and ritual. Allah is God. Jesus is a prophet of God, but he is not the head of the Moorish faith. In addition, Jesus is an "Asiatic," i. e., a member of the dark-skinned group; only by means of a deliberate distortion of the racial background of Jesus was it possible for Europeans (whites) to claim him as one of their own and establish him as the head of their church. (Compare Hitler's Asiatic "Aryans.") The usual Christian rites are absent. There is no conversion, sanctification, or unusual experience. Heaven is a figure of the mind, and Moors believe that they make their own heaven while on this earth. Death is a normal phenomenon in the natural scheme of things, and to be taken in stride as a step in the process of attaining to Allah. There is, accordingly, a life after death, and the reincarnation of the prophet, Noble Drew Ali, suggests that there is more than one life on this earth. There is also a belief that the turning point of the present system on earth will be the year 2000. Christmas and Easter are not celebrated as the Christians celebrate these, but there are analogous celebrations commemorating the birth and reincarnation of the prophet.

Summary Evaluation of Moorish Science Temple of America

CONFORMITY WITH ORTHODOX EVANGELICAL PATTERN

There is practically no conformity, except that for God we may substitute Allah, and that Jesus is recognized as a prophet of God. There is also a millennial concept which follows closely the pattern of some evangelical and holiness churches, but I have no details as to its apocalyptic implications, if any.

DEVIATIONS FROM ORTHODOX EVANGELICAL PATTERN

Allah is God.
Jesus (Mohammed, Noble Drew Ali) is God's prophet.
Rites: No baptism, Holy Communion
Holy Day: Friday and not Sunday
No conversion
Heaven is in the mind (no hell).
Music is very rudimentary (compare Quakers).

Segregation of sexes in place of worship
Sacred text: *Holy Koran* of Noble Drew Ali

THE CULTS COMPARED AMONG THEMSELVES

A summary survey of similarities and differences among the cults discloses the following:

Religious Faith
> *Christian:* Mt. Sinai, United House of Prayer
> *Modified Judaism:* Church of God
> *Moslem:* Moorish Science Temple
> *Christian Eclectic:* Father Divine Peace Mission

Sacred Text
> *Bible:* Mt. Sinai, United House of Prayer, Father Divine (?)
> *Talmud:* Church of God
> *New Day:* Father Divine
> *Holy Koran* of Noble Drew Ali: Moorish Science Temple

Beliefs and Practices
> *Conversion:* Mt. Sinai, United House of Prayer, Church of God, Father Divine
> *Sanctification:* Mt. Sinai, United House of Prayer, Church of God, Father Divine
> *Unusual Experience:* Mt. Sinai, United House of Prayer, Father Divine
> *Millennium:* All
> *Baptism:* Mt. Sinai, United House of Prayer, Church of God
> *Holy Communion:* Mt. Sinai, United House of Prayer, Father Divine (?)

Sabbaths
> *Friday:* Moorish Science Temple
> *Saturday:* Church of God
> *Sunday:* Mt. Sinai, United House of Prayer, Father Divine

Days of Worship
> *Sunday, Wednesday, Friday:* Moorish Science Temple
> *Sunday, Wednesday, Friday, Saturday:* Church of God
> *All days:* Mt. Sinai, United House of Prayer, Father Divine

Observance of Christian Festal Days (Christmas-Easter)
> Mt. Sinai, United House of Prayer

Spiritual Healing
> Mt. Sinai, United House of Prayer, Church of God (?), Father Divine, Moorish Science Temple (?)

Limitation of Marriage

   No marriage: Father Divine
   By endogamy: Mt. Sinai, United House of Prayer (?), Church of God, Moorish Science Temple

Racial Endogamy

   Church of God, Moorish Science Temple

Divorce

   Taboo: Mt. Sinai, United House of Prayer, Father Divine
   Conditional: Church of God, Moorish Science Temple under special conditions

Taboos

   Fornication: All
   Adultery: All
   Lying: All
   Stealing: All
   Backbiting: All
   Straightening the Hair: All (United House of Prayer possibly excepted)
   Impure conversation: All
   Profanity: All (Prophet Cherry himself excepted)
   Indulgence in Athletic Games: All
   Attending games, motion pictures, etc.: All
   Drinking intoxicants: All except the Church of God where practice is expressly encouraged.
   Polishing the Nails: All except United House of Prayer
   Use of racial names: Church of God, Father Divine, Moorish Science Temple
   Wearing Short Dresses: All
   Chewing gum: All
   Gambling: All
   Eating pork: Church of God, Moorish Science Temple
   Photographs: Church of God
   Marriage: Father Divine
   Divorce: Mt. Sinai, United House of Prayer, Father Divine

Concept of Heaven

   Far away: Mt. Sinai, United House of Prayer
   On earth: Father Divine
   In mind: Moorish Science Temple
   Three different heavens: Church of God

Speaking in Tongues

   Mt. Sinai, United House of Prayer, Father Divine (?)

Segregation of Sexes in Place of Worship
Mt. Sinai, United House of Prayer, Father Divine (?)

Dancing
Frenzied: Mt. Sinai, United House of Prayer, Father Divine
Moderate (in situ): Church of God
No dancing: Moorish Science Temple

Music
With Instruments: Mt. Sinai, United House of Prayer, Church of God, Father Divine
Chants (without instruments): Moorish Science Temple

Male Headdress Worn during Services
Church of God, Moorish Science Temple

Worship of Leader
Father Divine and the United House of Prayer
Church of God and Moorish Science Temple revere leaders and look up to them as prophets of God.

Racial Emphasis; Membership
Church of God, Moorish Science Temple

Interracial Emphasis; Membership
Father Divine

Emphasis on Name
Church of God, Moorish Science Temple

Name of Place of Worship
Church: Mt. Sinai, Father Divine
House of Prayer: Church of God, United House of Prayer
Temple: Moorish Science Temple

Nomenclature of Members
Brothers and Sisters: All

Prayer to East during Worship
Church of God, Moorish Science Temple

Enterprises developing out of Community Life of Cults
Stores: All except United House of Prayer
Objects for sale in place of worship: United House of Prayer, Father Divine (*New Day*)

VIII

WHY THE CULT ATTRACTS

WHAT is there about the cult which draws to it the thousands of adherents from our large northern centers?

As is to be expected, different people are attracted to a cult for different reasons. This fact is reflected in a difference in emphasis in the various cults. But there is one main attraction which stands out in all cults, making a kind of common bond among them: it is the desire to get closer to some supernatural power, be it God, the Holy Spirit, or Allah.

From the testimony of members of the various cults,[1] it becomes clear that another compelling factor is relief from physical or mental illness. Race consciousness, or nationalism, is marked in two of the cults, while in the Father Divine Peace Mission the consideration of race and its international implications courses through the entire fabric of belief and practice. To these, of course, must be added the compelling personality of the leader.

These four compulsions, then—the supernatural being, the personality of the leader, relief from physical and mental illness, and race consciousness—appear to be most prominent factors in the respective attractions which these cults have for their members.

SUDDENNESS OF APPEAL

It often happens that the individual is directed unexpectedly to the cult by some dramatic experience, as when an ill person is suddenly and miraculously healed. Such a person will date his advent into the cult from that moment. Thus an oriental member of Father Divine's Peace Mission testified to me: "My woman was sick with cancer. The doctors had given her up altogether. I went over to Sayville with her to Father Divine's. He healed her right away. Since then my woman and I have been members."

This man, when further questioned, referred to Father Divine's "goodness," his "greatness," his wonderful spirit of unity which

---

[1] See Appendix A.

was always breaking down the bars of racial discrimination. But uppermost in his mind was the dramatic moment when his "woman" was healed.

A member of the Moorish Science Temple invariably emphasizes the racial aspect of his cult. The compulsion of racial identity is uppermost. Nevertheless, he is likely to confide later that through the prophet he, or someone dear to him, was healed of mental, physical, or financial distress.

Mt. Sinai is interested primarily in the search for "truth," getting near to the Holy Spirit, leading the evangelical life.

The United House of Prayer also speaks eloquently and emphatically for the "holy life," but this usually is expressed in terms of devotion to the leader. A frequent response to the question, "What do you get from following the teachings of the United House of Prayer?" was, "We are trying to find the right way, and Daddy Grace knows the way."

A study of the various statements made by members in their testimonies bears out these observations. Thus:

W. G. was impressed by Prophet Cherry's disdain of everything containing the word "Negro." He despises gentiles (whites). He was ripe for a nationalistic cult.

* * *

H. R. had lost faith in Christianity when he was a boy. He hated to see his mother get "happy." He loathed the hypocrisy of the Christians. He joined the Moslems.

* * *

H. C. was mentally sick and too poor to go to college. He found his place in the Mt. Sinai Holy Church.

* * *

X. Y. Z. was studying for the ministry. He wanted to be a religious teacher, but he could not reconcile Christian teaching and practice. He became a Moslem.

* * *

J. H. joined Mt. Sinai Holy Church because his wife had already become a member. She had wanted to "get nearer to the Holy Spirit," and he did not want to be inferior to his wife in his closeness to the same spirit.

* * *

Redeemed Love despaired of walking again. Someone said, "Father Divine!" The thought bore down upon her. Suddenly she was healed. Thus she became a Divinite, and through her other members of her family joined.

* * *

C. C. believed that only through Daddy Grace could one get into the Kingdom. Naturally, also, Daddy Grace can heal the sick, and give sight to the blind.

* * *

A woman who has been floundering in Christian belief, and become mentally distressed by the paradoxes of American Christian practice, especially where Negroes are involved, suddenly learns of a group which can teach her her proper name. She joins the Moorish Science Temple.

* * *

The story unfolds in this manner until the repetition becomes stereotyped.

IS THIS APPEAL DIFFERENT FROM ORDINARY APPEAL?

Naturally there will be those who will ask: But does this process which leads people into the cult differ essentially from that which attracts people to the more orthodox evangelical churches? Do not these orthodox churches draw their members for similar reasons?

Certainly the more orthodox churches do not explicitly state their appeals in such terms as these. While such churches profess to bring their followers closer to the Holy Spirit, it is rare that we find them proclaiming salvation through a knowledge of one's racial identity, or promising eternal grace through the healing of the body or mind (as contrasted with the soul), or through setting one's personal business problems in order.

It should be remembered also that most of the people whose testimonies have been utilized for the observations and conclusions made in this study had previously been members of some of the more orthodox denominations. Thus, among eighteen members of the United House of Prayer who were questioned with regard to their original beliefs (all eighteen had come out of the South), fourteen had been Baptists, two Methodists, and only two had never belonged to a church previously. Most of them had made their connection with the United House of Prayer in Philadelphia. A survey of other testimonies substantiates this example.

Mays and Nicholson, in their splendid study of the Negro church, have advanced reasons why Negroes from southern rural areas tend to seek small groups when they come North or go off to the cities. Their observations appear to be borne out in the attraction of the cult.

For example:

A man in Detroit, deacon in a store-front church, told one of the workers that he could not pray in a big church. Further inquiry into the meaning of the statement revealed that the deacon really meant that he could not pray in the big Detroit church as he was accustomed to praying in the rural church in the South. His long, loud prayer would not be in place in the semi-sophisticated Detroit church. Therefore he organized a church of his own.

Also:

In Detroit, a pastor of a house church told one of the writers how he happened to organize a church. He stated that he talked with a large number of southern people who desired a church similar in worship to churches in the rural South. As a minister, this man felt obliged to start a church for these people. He expressed the conviction that many Negroes in Detroit, formerly faithful church members in the South, had suffered moral and religious shipwreck because they could not make the necessary adjustment, and the resident Christians did not always have the requisite sympathy, imagination, and resourcefulness to make them feel at home, and to introduce them gradually to the new ways of life and thought. An hour's interview with the pastor disclosed the fact that for forty years he had been a leader in the rural South—pastor, moderator of conventions and associations, and a big man in his lodge; now he was suddenly thrust into an environment in which leadership in church and other areas was so completely monopolized that he could hardly hope to be the leader he once was. It is not to be wondered at that this man organized a church in his house. These psychological factors are not only basic elements in discussing the effect of migration on the increase in the number of urban churches, but basic also in a consideration of the increase of church membership in the urban areas. Many members of store-front and house churches would forsake the church altogether if the big churches were the only reliance.[2]

According to Mays' and Nicholson's figures,[3] the increase of holiness groups in northern centers far surpasses that in the South from which the Negroes migrated originally. This might be considered an obvious outcome of the movement of large num-

[2] Mays and Nicholson, *op. cit.*, p. 98 ff.
[3] Figures are for the period *ca.* 1932.

bers of Negroes from the South to the North; but this cannot be the fundamental reason, inasmuch as the bulk of Negro population still resides in the South.

It seems reasonable to believe that the striking increase of cult groups in the large northern centers is to be related in part to the psychological factors which are implied, first in a change from rural to urban life, and second in the adjustment of mental attitudes to new mores, especially with regard to the rights of men of different races, as these vary between the North and South.

The rural life in the South and, relatively speaking, southern urban life as well, is much less complicated and nerve-racking than life in the North. The Negro, accustomed to the southern mores, and used to living chiefly to himself in a segregated scheme of life, has relatively few adjustments to make so far as his relations with white folk are concerned.[4]

In the North, much of the old accustomed way of life has been shattered. Not only is the erstwhile southern Negro embarrassed by the presence of thousands of "sophisticated" Negroes who want no reminders of "back-home" ways, but the infinitely more baffling problem of making a new adjustment to life as a relatively free man, and consequently having to meet free competition (instead of the paternalistic regard so commonly manifested towards Negroes by white people in the South) are more than this type of Negro is able to cope with easily, after the experience of many years in the South.

It must come as a great relief as well as release to such people to enter into the spirit of a group like one of the holiness cults, with its offer of assurance through grace and sanctification, and the knowledge that they will be aided not only in their efforts to support their customary burdens, but that in addition they will be equipped to measure arms with the white man, something

[4] Studies of caste situations in the South have shown the rigidity of much of the psychological conditioning of Negroes in their relations with whites. Thus, in the lower-class Negro Hopkins family in Louisiana, we are told, ". . . they have learned to adjust to their color-caste subordination. Their policy may be stated in a word: 'submit'—to all but the most violent and most direct of physical assaults. When Mary Hopkins was asked how she felt about being colored, she said, 'I don't mind being jes' like Gawd made me. . . .' Asked if she minded riding in the back of the bus, she said, 'I jes' go on to the back. That's the place they got for us. You don't never get in trouble like that!' . . . Mrs. Hopkins has carefully instructed Mary in caste etiquette as she understands it. Mary is to avoid temptations to fight white people. 'Don't pay any attention, come on home—sit in the rear of the bus 'cause that's their bus anyhow!' "—Allison Davis and John Dollard, *Children of Bondage*, pp. 65, 66.

they scarcely dreamed of doing previous to their advent into the North.

Here, for example, is a significant piece of testimony by such a cult member in New York City, who under great provocation nevertheless conquered her impulse to react in a way which for most of us would have been very natural and normal:

I am glad to testify to my Father that He has kept me spotless and sinless during the week. I am glad I am holy and sanctified, because if I wasn't I know that I would have fallen down long before this. In fact I would have been out of a job this very week if I was not sanctified, because when my Madam came in the room and said some mighty nasty things to me, I had a mind to tell her just where she got off, and if the Old Adam had been in me I would have given that Madam such a tongue-lashing as she never had in her life. But sweet Jesus was in my heart. I did not say anything to the woman, but merely said deep down within myself, "Sweet Jesus, stay with me. Keep me holy and pure. You had to die on the cross, and I know I can stand this for your sake." And then it all blew over and everything was just fine.

In the Deep South, this Negro woman probably would not have had such a mental conflict; for since the relations between the races do not approximate even the nominal equality of the North, she would have been conditioned psychologically and emotionally to accept more readily the carping attitudes of her mistress.

If the question is asked why such an individual does not enter an orthodox evangelical church rather than one of the cults, the answer is that in many cases he does affiliate himself with a Baptist or Methodist group, but in other instances the cult, for reasons indicated in this study, is more attractive. Hence one is led to believe that, for many of their members, certain religious cults in northern urban communities assist the transplanted southern worshipper, accustomed to the fixed racial mores and caste requirements of the South, to adjust his psychological and emotional reactions to conditions in the North, where all life and living are more fluid and intermingling of the races is inevitable.[5]

THE HOLINESS CULT A KIND OF GRADUATE CHURCH

The cult communicant frequently remarks, "To belong to this church (or temple) is to go a step higher." He means that

[5] One gets this impression very definitely in those cults which possess considerable political motivation, namely, Father Divine, Moorish Science Temple of America, and Black Jews.

by joining the cult he has got closer to the fount of all knowledge and wisdom.   In other words, joining the cult is a new experience not altogether unlike the conversion which originally brought him into the evangelical church.[6]

The holiness cults in particular emphasize that it is not sufficient for one that he has been converted.   After conversion one must be sanctified; and besides, he must be filled with the Holy Spirit.[7]

For many, then, the cult is a graduate church; like the university it may be said to offer a master's and a doctor's degree in addition to the bachelor's degree.   To become one of the elect you must have experienced all three.

Thus the cult offers a haven to many baffled and disillusioned church-goers (as well as to that stream of Negro life which carries on a mere desultory acquaintance with the evangelical church) who actually have become fearful that mere belief in Christianity, or mere church attendance, will not bring them to the promised land.

They crave a deeper insight into the mystery of evangelical religion; they need new experiences.   Having attended church at some time or other among ordinary converts, many of whom had little else to show than the "bachelor's degree" testifying to their original conversion, they are convinced now that something more is necessary in their earthly lives in order that they may be certain to enjoy the hereafter.

True, the pastor has told them often about the saving grace of the Blood and the Lamb, about death-bed repentance, and the

[6] Although the masculine pronoun is used when referring to cult members, actually the membership in all of the cults, the Moors possibly excepted, is predominantly feminine.   An investigation needs to be made for the purpose of ascertaining how much the participation of many of the women in the cults results from conditions in the home, where perhaps husbands have lost interest in the family life, and the children, who identify themselves with a more modern age, have wandered off.

[7] Herskovits in *The Myth of the Negro Past* emphasizes the analogy of "spirit possession," i. e., the unusual experience, to a similar phenomenon in West African religious practice, and this, he believes, is an important clue in the quest for African survivals in American Negro religious worship.   However, the average Negro holiness worshipper lays great emphasis on sanctification, i. e., the pure life, and although he will stipulate that the unusual experience (spirit possession) is necessary to salvation, it is the concern with living purely and in a holy manner which occupies his everyday thought.   Once you have had the unusual experience, you have had it, and that is that.   The pure life (sanctification) is a matter of constant preoccupation, and can be shattered at any time even after years and years of adherence to the holiness principles.   Any sermon in a holiness church, or discussion with holiness folk will disclose the overwhelming importance attached to the pure life.

power of Jesus to save the most hardened criminal, but these people require something which is personally more reassuring. Scores of cult members interviewed for this study manifested this concern.   They find reassurance in the cult.

There they are impressed with the opportunity to strive for the second degree of the Christian life, sanctification.   Undoubtedly in part because opportunity to participate in many of the normal activities of life which enrich the experience of white Americans is limited or circumscribed, these folk become intensely devoted to their religious pursuit.[8]   Eagerly they endeavor to shed all carnal predispositions and desires, in order that they may present themselves before God and man sanctified and pure.

But even these are not yet saved.   They are taught that only a limited number of people on earth will be saved in the last days.   This excludes many who have been converted, and it can exclude even members of the cult who have striven to live pure and sanctified lives, submerging every carnal obsession, refraining from drinking intoxicants, from smoking, dancing with members of the opposite sex, swearing, going to ball games, gambling, using profane language, and from doing just about everything and anything which might make ordinary life bearable.

To be among the elect you must reach the third stage of salvation, namely, become filled with the Holy Spirit; and the test of this is some unusual experience—in some of the cults an evidence of the ability to speak in tongues, but in others merely an extraordinary occurrence, such as a vision or a dream, hearing a heavenly voice, or a miraculous healing.

THE RÔLE OF MUSIC IN THE CULT

If one were to be guided solely by the testimonies in evaluating the elements of the cult which make it attractive to followers,

[8] The question will be raised: If Negroes react in this way because as a racial group they find their outlets of expression restricted, why is it that southern whites who are not circumscribed by these racial taboos also give evidence that they are more emotionally tied to religion than their brethren in the North?   The answer obviously is that vast numbers of southern whites are more restricted emotionally and otherwise than northern whites, just as people in rural areas usually are more restricted than those who live in metropolitan districts.   Even in flourishing southern cities like Atlanta and Memphis there is not the degree of cultural stimulation for the masses in music, opera, forums, and the theatre which is to be found in the great northern centers such as New York, Boston, Philadelphia, Chicago, or San Francisco.   As for the outlying southern areas, the cultural barrenness is too well known to need comment.

music scarcely would enter into consideration. But unquestionably one of the most compelling forces in the cult is its music.

Were it not for the Moors, the author would be inclined to posit it as a fact that where there is no music there is no Negro cult. Having observed services in the Moorish Science Temple of America over a period of years, it is clear to me that here is an example of cult worship which proves that a Negro cult can persist without the compelling power of music and its rhythms, harmonies, and dissonances, as well as with an absence of shouting and other signs of emotionalism usually associated with Negro cult life in America.[9]

But in each of the other cults, and in every Negro cult I have ever observed, except the Moors, music is a prime feature of the entire performance. This is true to such a degree that the author has frequently observed the whole religious performance fall flat because there was not the proper kind or volume of music to set a certain tone for the communicants; on the other hand enervated services can be completely transformed by the injection of a song.

Often there is only a piano to accompany the singing. An interesting thing about the player is that he usually picks up the melody according to the key of the singers, reversing the practice in the orthodox churches, where the instrumentalist first gives the key and the singers follow. The first method makes for infinitely greater spontaneity in the singing.

Frequently there are additional instruments. At Rockland Palace there is an orchestra of twenty or more pieces, mixed both

---

[9] Frazier, *The Negro Family in the United States,* has the following to say about isolated Negro family groups, usually mixed in blood, which he studied in their isolated locales in various parts of the United States: ". . . these families of mixed blood have influenced the behaviour of the Negro in other ways. The children in such families generally exhibit the restraint and self-discipline which have distinguished their forbears. For example, this may be seen even in their religious services which have been free from the extreme emotionalism of the Negro masses. In fact, when a Negro minister with religious background of the masses has occasionally been assigned to these communities, he has been forced to modify his mode of preaching to be acceptable to their pattern of religious worship."—p. 245. The members of the Moorish Science Temple appear to be purer Negro types than the groups referred to by Frazier, but they are very similar with regard to a psychological isolationism which their form of religious worship develops and encourages. It may be said of members of this cult that they form racial islands in the urban communities where they are to be found. (Do not confuse the "Moors" of this cult with the "Moors" to whom Frazier refers when he speaks of one of the "racial-island" groups to be found in Delaware. These people of Algonkian Indian origin are the subject of a recent book, *Delaware's Forgotten Folk,* by C. A. Weslager, University of Pennsylvania Press.)

as to sex and race, and consisting of piano, horns of various kinds, drums, tambourines and castanets, guitars, and banjos. Besides these, the young Rosebuds, a group of girls, have developed a chorus of unusual charm, which performs usually to the accompaniment of the piano.

In the United House of Prayer dependence is placed on the piano, but this frequently is augmented. At times the piano is not used at all, and then the drum or tambourine takes the lead.

The Church of God has an orchestra (without piano), including one or two violins.

At Mt. Sinai the music usually consists of piano and drum. There is a choir also.

In all these services, music is employed not merely to preface or conclude, or even to relieve the program; it is the backbone of the service itself, even including the performance of the preacher or chief speaker. It is an unusual service if, somewhere in the chief speaker's discourse, he does not interrupt his remarks with music of some kind, with singing, an instrument, dancing, or the clapping of the hands by the members of the congregation.

In the Mt. Sinai Holy Church the author has observed the interpolation of song and dance by the chief speaker, usually a woman, as often as six times in a single sermon. Prophet Cherry beats a huge bass drum. Father Divine will rock on his heels as he sits, and sometimes he breaks out extemporaneously into song. Bishop Grace likes to stand up while the band or orchestra is playing and, seizing a fan, pretend that he is strumming a guitar or ukulele.

Such music is not intended merely to entertain or heighten the interest in the performance; it is not an attraction in the ordinary sense of the term; it is a compelling force. Thus, when in the Father Divine service the chorus suddenly bursts forth with

> Father Divine's love will get you even if you do watch out,
> And when it does, you will sing and shout!

the outsider really is being warned that if he is not very careful, he is going to be carried away by the music, by the rhythmical cadences of the song of the moment. Undoubtedly many converts to the cult have been won over at just such a moment. To an observer, it is apparent that spirit possession is a common occurrence under this compulsion.

THE COMPULSION OF THE ESOTERIC

Finally, the cult heightens a sense of the esoteric within the group. This apparently is a satisfying experience for members of the group. The intensity of this feeling varies with the cult.

Some observers have indicated that this esoteric sense tends to make the cult members unfriendly to those who are outside the group. The author's personal experiences are at variance with these observations. The one possible exception is the Moorish Science Temple, where members obviously are taught to regard all strangers with suspicion.

Undoubtedly there is acute awareness of kinship within the cult, but this does not serve to dampen or chill the friendly atmosphere where outsiders are concerned. Perhaps it depends on the attitude of the stranger. My experience has been that an open, friendly, and sympathetic, but not condescending, attitude invariably is rewarded with equal warmth and friendliness. This has been the case even in the Moorish Science Temple where, because of the secret nature of the cult, only a certain amount of consideration can be given to strangers. One is almost tempted to suggest that the friendliness of members of the cult towards strangers is to be classified among the factors which attract outsiders to the cult.

IX

THE CULT AS A FUNCTIONAL INSTITUTION

REFERENCE has been made to the rôle of the Negro cult in relieving and releasing psychological tensions, particularly in the case of Negroes who are confronted for the first time with the problems of northern urban life. It would be natural for cult leaders to recognize the functional possibilities of the cult mechanism along various lines; in fact it would be difficult for them to eschew the temptation to accomplish various ends by means of the cult which under a different social order in our country would appertain to more secular institutions.

We are not surprised therefore to observe a diversity of activities in some of the cults which undoubtedly reflects such recognition on the part of the leading members. To express this tendency in more technical terms, it would appear that the normal social needs of the members of some of these groups, and particularly the need of leadership-expression in its various forms by the leaders and the more aggressive members of the cults, become transformed into derived cultural necessities and imperatives.[1]

Here again the differences in conditions of life for the individual Negro in the North and in the South appear to be reflected in the corresponding development of his institutional life. In the South it is not unusual to encounter Negroes who have amassed considerable wealth in business, particularly in real estate and insurance, in the trades, and in the professions. Since for them there is little cultural life, the resourceful Negroes are likely to engage in activities which prove economically fruitful.[2]

---

[1] In the discussion of the cult as a functional institution, I am using the term in the sense in which it is employed by Malinowski. Cf. his article, "Group and the Individual in Functional Analysis," *American Journal of Sociology*, XLIV (May 1939), 938–64.

[2] John Dollard, in his valuable study *Caste and Class in a Southern Town*, has indicated the ways in which Negroes in the South are exploited economically by the white group, frequently reaching so far as to eliminate competition by the Negro middleman. Nevertheless it is almost a truism that until recently, with the concentration of enormous numbers of Negroes in northern metropolitan areas, the most significant economic strides by Negroes have been in the South.

In the North, however, the competition of the white man narrowly restricts the Negro even within the limits of his own racial group, while the economic barriers outside the group are only slightly lower than those in the South. Consequently the Negro in the North, when compared with the Negro in the South, often appears to be "all head and no body." That is to say, the Negro in the North frequently has a much better intellectual equipment than his southern brother, but in the absence of avenues of employment and lucrative revenue, he becomes an economic and political slave.

It cannot be without significance, therefore, that movements like the Father Divine Peace Mission Movement are characterized by a diversity of activities, notably in the economic, political, and educational spheres, which tend to compensate for the paucity of analogous activities in life outside the cult.[3]

It is interesting to note that, in each of the five cults considered in this study, evidence in varying degrees is forthcoming of an awareness by the leadership of the need to take up the economic, educational, and political slack which is a significant feature of Negro life even in the North. This is certainly not accidental, as the prevalence of the phenomenon within these cults is general, and in several instances it reaches very large proportions.

MT. SINAI HOLY CHURCH

If we begin with the relatively minor expression of this tendency as we observe it in the Mt. Sinai Holy Church, we note at least three evidences of these functional characteristics:

[3] It is necessary to reiterate that the recognition of these needs lies chiefly, and sometimes solely, in the leaders of the groups, though, as will become more apparent in the further exposition of the Father Divine cult, this sense of recognition may be diffused through the membership generally. This is indicated in the testimonies of members, particularly in the Father Divine and Prophet Cherry cults. But in another sense the recognition even by the leaders is merely an indication of the functional rôle of the cult mechanism itself. It is because the leader is unique that he and not someone else organizes or develops a cult; later the cult, functioning by means of his leadership, comes to be recognized by the leader, or leaders, as a vehicle for transforming social needs into cultural imperatives. If it seems to be granting the leader too great perspicacity to be a part of such recognition, the argument for the functional rôle of the cult is not weakened on that account; the actual fact would seem to be that the leader at this point is as much constrained by the functional tendencies of the cult mechanism as he was originally to establish the cult itself. That many members of the cult are unaware of these implications (or even if, for that matter, the leader himself does not recognize the fact) is not a reason for denying that the institution which has been organized impels the leader to operate in these channels.

For a number of years a private school of elementary grade status was provided for the children of the cult. Because of certain difficulties with the city laws governing such schools it has been closed recently, but plans are under way to revive the institution at the large model farm in New Jersey, a second functional derivative where, in a kind of coöperative project, revenue is raised out of the tilling of the soil for general farm produce, for feeding the poor, providing alms, and aiding the sick. The third instance is the rather pretentious home used by Bishop Robinson as her Philadelphia residence, which also is a kind of hospice for various women of her flock. Here, from time to time, members may live in a state of ease and comfort to which they are not accustomed, and which it would be impossible for them to purchase in the open market since such a commodity is not readily available to Negroes. Presumably the expense of this practice comes out of the general financial intake. More recently there has been talk of opening a bath and health resort at Hot Springs, Arkansas.

THE UNITED HOUSE OF PRAYER

In the United House of Prayer for All People (Bishop Grace), the same economic functionalism is discernible. In the sale of soaps, perfumes, and stationery, there may be absent the noble striving for national integration, so prominent in the cult of the Black Jews or the racial fanaticism of the Moorish Americans; nevertheless we have here an example of an urge which, because it is caught up in the paradoxes of the peculiar racial dichotomy, seeks to find its way through perhaps the only clear channel reserved to it, namely the religious channel.

A Woolworth or a Rockefeller operates in a secular field which, according to the mores of his culture, is wide open to him. It may not be pertinent to compare Bishop Grace with these gentlemen, but the pattern of his economic activities does not differ greatly from that of numerous entrepreneurs who exploit the possibilities of various media in order to turn a financial profit. To the student of functional determinants, such economic strivings are no less respectable than are the beginnings of many other economic efforts in the past which emerged from their earlier history of tawdriness and lack of respectability.[4]

---

[4] In passing, it is interesting to note that many of the magnates in the secular world reversed the Bishop Grace process by becoming ardent sponsors of the Christian church after they had achieved material success.

CHURCH OF GOD

In the Church of God (Black Hebrews), Prophet Cherry constantly emphasizes the poverty of the black race, and their failure to acquire worldly goods. As a result, there has been a tendency for his followers to go into business for themselves. The prophet owns a vegetable store and a butcher shop. Other followers have opened shoe repair shops, restaurants, tailor shops, and cleaning and dyeing establishments. Some of these ventures have failed. Still the principle holds true that an economic need recognized by virtually all Negroes has been met to some degree by an institutionalized program on the part of these followers. Since there is a strong feeling of kinship within the group, there is a tendency to support these economic ventures.

Because of the unusual character of the prophet's religious teachings, a special school is held on Monday nights, when Hebrew is taught. Small children as well as adults appear in these classes. The members of the cult are made aware constantly of the fact that an educational program designed to meet their special needs as Black Jews, instead of the educational program of the public schools, is essential.

MOORISH SCIENCE TEMPLE

We noted in our consideration of the Moors how the members of this cult ran into difficulties when its leaders attempted to exploit the economic possibilities of the cult through sales of various articles and nostrums. In some of the cities, business enterprises such as grocery stores and shoe repair shops were established. These have not been very successful, due partly to the relatively small number of members in the respective branches of the cult, and partly to the fact that frequently these members live in scattered sections of their metropolitan communities. The fact is, however, that out of the foundation laid by religious activity, other activities developed which were designed to fill economic and social needs of the group.

In Philadelphia, attempts have been made to open a school in place of the public schools. This is the result of several factors in the cult life:

1. General dissatisfaction with "European" training, and a sense of need for a kind of education which will more nearly guarantee the development of the individual into "racially" conscious Moorish Americans.

2. Friction that occurs because Moorish-American children are distinct from other children because of the fez and certain customs.

3. A sense of separateness which the cult habits engender. Thus the failure to wear neckties brings the children into conflict with teachers who insist upon "proper" dress. The bearded faces of the fathers and their incomplete neckgear, as well as the severe dress of the mothers, have nurtured rumors of untidiness and even uncleanliness to which the members are very sensitive.

One interesting feature of the cults considered thus far is a predilection for uniformed club groups, or distinctiveness in the dress of the members. Many of the smaller organizational units of these cults are uniformed, and in the Church of God and the United House of Prayer there are groups of men who wear military dress and carry swords. The reaction of the outsider may be to smile at these manifestations, and perhaps to ascribe them to the "childlike" nature of the Negro which is attracted to uniforms, baubles, and the like. To what extent, we wonder, does this demonstration serve as a compensation for the reluctance of most branches of our armed services, as well as auxiliary organizations like the Red Cross, where uniforms are cherished, to include a normal complement of Negroes within the ranks? [5]

FATHER DIVINE PEACE MISSION MOVEMENT

It is when we come to the Father Divine Peace Mission Movement that the function of the cult to transform social needs by means of secular enterprises is most clearly demonstrated. Here these transformations achieve a plane of efficiency and a scope which in some instances lift them clear of the realm of amateurism, and establish them with those other secular expressions in America which have culminated in the concept of "big business."

Perhaps the only substantial difference, morphologically, between the functional forms which have developed in this movement and those forms which have been produced in the ordinary processes of big business in our country, is that in the Father Divine Peace Mission Movement these forms are functional by-products rather than end-products.

Many critics who see in the Father Divine Peace Mission Movement nothing but a "racket" probably miss this important func-

---

[5] As a result of increasing insistence by Negroes, representation has been provided in the Marines, Navy, WACS, etc., to a degree unknown before the present emergency.

tional implication. Such people, observing that many patrons of the Peace restaurants and of the three-cent (without tips) shoe shine parlors are not members of the cult, opine that these secular expressions should in no way be related to the religious expression.

It is true that many people who benefit by the functions of the movement have no vital interest in the movement itself, but this probably has no more significance than the fact that most people using an electric light bulb for reading purposes have no knowledge of or interest in the processes by which the lamp was created. The essential fact is that out of an attempt, through the Father Divine Peace Mission Movement, to resolve a need of a segment of humanity, numerous significant functional transformations have ensued.

A perusal of the advertisements in a recent copy of the *New Day* confirms the point. More than fifty of these advertisements are of business establishments which are directly or indirectly connected with the Peace Mission Movement. It is to be assumed that there are many more such establishments controlled by individuals and groups which have not advertised in the *New Day*.

Among the enterprises advertised in this particular issue are the following: automobile accessories and repairs; garages; cabinet makers; coal, ice, oil distributors; barbers; free employment agency; express and hauling; food distribution; jewelry; women's wear; laundries; notions; radios and repair; restaurants; shoe repair; tailors and cleaners.

The most spectacular economic function of the Father Divine Peace Mission Movement develops out of its real estate holdings. The "extensions," of which there are scores, are really hotels. This is of the utmost significance in the life of Negroes, for, quite apart from the item of expense in which these hotels are distinguished by the amazingly low cost of services rendered (usually two dollars a week room rent, and fifteen cents a meal with no tips allowed), the significant fact lies in this: here we have a functional transformation with regard to a very vital need of American Negroes growing out of the general practice of American hostelries to refuse to receive them.

To a degree probably unknown or unsuspected by people outside the racial group, the psychology of an entire race, numbering nearly fifteen million people, has been conditioned by this need. White Americans look forward to travel as one of life's richest boons; but the American Negro contemplates travel in the United States with a degree of misgiving amounting to dread. A Negro, when setting out on a trip, either must have every stop-over very carefully arranged in advance, or he must see to it that he does not arrive at an unknown place too late in the evening to shop around for accommodations; otherwise he is likely to be compelled to spend the night out of doors and without anything to eat.

It would seem that this need should have been met many years ago, but little has developed to ameliorate this condition. Now, however, the Father Divine Peace Mission Movement, a religious undertaking, is in the process of meeting such a need through the functional transformation described above. It is hardly to be wondered at that the name "Promised Land" has been bestowed upon the choicest of these extensions located in the beautiful Hudson River Valley and the Catskill Mountains.[6]

How the Father Divine Peace Mission Movement functions in an analogous manner on the political-economic plane is demon-

[6] When the Father Divine Peace Mission Movement purchased the extension at Krum Elbow, across the river from the Hyde Park residence of President Roosevelt, a cartoonist on the Chicago *Daily News* thought to enliven his sheet with a drawing with the title "At Krum Elbow."

He pictured a little black urchin standing with hat in hand on President Roosevelt's doorstep at Hyde Park. Two empty milk bottles still remained at the doorstep of the President's house, one of them containing the usual message to the milkman. The President of the United States was pictured coatless, standing behind a screen door and looking even more perplexed than might have been the case had he been confronted suddenly by a troop of Nazi parachuters. The Negro boy is calling up to him, "Father Divine wants t' know kin he borry yo' lawn-mo?" Below the cartoon is another caption which reads, "DON'T FORGET YOUR GOOD NEIGHBOR POLICY, FRANKLIN!"

In this connection it is of interest to note also that the man who recently was elected president of the North and South American Hotel Keepers' Association, a cultural organization for the promotion of hemispherical good-will, is himself the manager of a well-known hotel in Harrisburg, Pennsylvania, against whom a suit was brought, under the Pennsylvania Equal Rights Act, for refusing to permit five Negroes in an interracial group to be served in the dining room of his hotel.

It should be remembered that properties owned by the Father Divine Peace Mission Movement in the Promised Land are only a small fraction of the real estate holdings of the movement, and do not include the immensely valuable parcels of real property in a score or more locations in New York City. *See* Richard S. Bird, in the *New York Times Magazine*, July 2, 1939. Since this study was made, the Father Divine Peace Mission Movement has purchased a pretentious hotel building located on the shore at Brigantine Beach, scarcely five minutes drive from Atlantic City. How religious and class lines break down in the face of an economic compulsion is clearly reflected in the clientele of this hotel, which includes Negroes from every social and occupational avenue of life. Note already has been made of increasing Philadelphia holdings.

strated in the following report by Floyd Calvin in the June 22, 1935, issue of the Pittsburgh *Courier,* a Negro weekly:

FATHER DIVINE THREATENS BOYCOTT AGAINST MILK COMPANIES—MAKES PROBE OF POLITICS TOWARDS RACE

It now looks like something more than the usual perfunctory gestures in Harlem's economic battles will come of the threatened boycott by Father Divine against milk companies if they don't employ colored drivers and mechanics. The "placating" letters sent to "Father" by Sheffield and Borden were promptly turned down when Divine replied that the companies had evaded the point—that they did not employ colored drivers and mechanics, which he specifically requested that they do. . . .

"Under further investigation, both within your stores and connections and especially with the public drivers on the streets of the city of New York and elsewhere, I do not find drivers non-discriminated according to your information given in your letter. If your concern is to be looked upon as equitable, we are looking forward for an immediate change in your staff of drivers on the public streets, especially in Harlem, by immediately placing 50% of a different color than what you now have."

These functional implications are again demonstrated in the Righteous Government program, which is the name of a specific effort within the movement to guide the entire politico-economic and educational motivation of the movement. The Righteous Government program was launched in January 1936, at a special convention of the followers of Father Divine called the International Righteous Government Convention. A Righteous Government platform was drawn up, which in addition to being a rare piece of legalistic exposition (containing as it does whole speeches by the leader) embraces nearly all the principles operative in the cult, and thereby points to its truly functional character:

1. The Righteous Government is to be interracial, international, interreligious, interdenominational, and non-partisan.
2. It is to be bound by the following principles:
    a. The entire human race is essentially one.
    b. Peace in the human race is to be established by eradicating prejudice, segregation and division among people, and promoting the welfare of every living creature.
    c. Equal opportunity for every individual without regard to race, creed, and color.

There are fourteen general planks. Of these, eight refer to injustices involving race, creed, and color. There are twelve purely economic planks and three educational provisions, also a special amendment calling for legislation "imposing the penalty for first degree murder on all members of lynch mobs killing or fatally injuring any person, together with a fine of Ten or Twenty Thousand Dollars to be paid by the county wherein the lynching occurs, to the estate of the injured or deceased person."

Thus the Father Divine Peace Mission Movement, which essentially is a religious organization, in effect becomes the mechanism by which various social urges, particularly those of its leaders and more socially dynamic members, may find outlets of expression. By making it possible for agencies to be established to fulfill these needs, it tends to transform these urges into the imperatives of American culture. It would appear that the Father Divine Peace Mission Movement outstrips the other cults in the extent to which it demonstrates these functional characteristics. This undoubtedly is due to a greater social awareness as well as a superior organizational capacity on the part of the leadership of the Father Divine Peace Mission Movement. Still it is clear that lurking within the framework of each of the cults are the seeds and roots of the same general tendency.

X

THE NEGRO AND HIS RELIGION

THE religiosity of the Negro often is taken for granted. Not only is this a popular opinion, but important social scientists intimate and even emphasize the fact.

To take two outstanding examples, there is the sociologist, Robert E. Park, who states,

I assume . . . the reason the Negro so readily and eagerly took over from the white man his heaven and his apocalyptic visions was because these materials met the demands of his peculiar *racial temperament* [italics mine]. . . .[1]

Herskovits, the anthropologist, has been quoted above as stating:

Underlying the life of the American Negro is a deep religious *bent* [italics mine] that is but the manifestation here of a similar drive that, everywhere in Negro societies, makes the supernatural a major focus of interest. The tenability of this position is apparent when it is considered how, in an age marked by skepticism, the Negro has held fast to belief. . . .

According to the same author, because religion is such a controlling factor in the life of the average Negro,

everywhere compensation in terms of the supernatural is . . . immediately acceptable to this underprivileged folk, and causes them, in contrast to other underprivileged groups elsewhere in the world, to turn to religion rather than to political action or other outlets for their frustration.[2]

The inference to be drawn from such opinions is that there is something in the Negro amounting almost to an inner compulsion which drives him into religious channels. Some facts and figures on the relation of the American Negro to his church, as compared with the relation of white people to their churches, might be suggestive in this connection.

[1] Park, *op. cit.,* p. 128.
[2] Herskovits, *Myth of the Negro Past,* p. 207.

In their highly revealing study of religion among American Negroes, Mays and Nicholson have disclosed that if we choose to be guided by the proportion of Negroes and whites in the United States who attend church, Negroes can scarcely be considered more religious than whites.[3]   Actually the proportion of white men attending church is higher than that for Negroes. The following figures refer to all church members in America over the age of thirteen years:

| Negro women: 73% | Negro men: 46% |
| White women: 62% | White men: 49% |

Thus it becomes apparent that more than 40 per cent of Negroes never attend church at all; and this compares with the total non-church going population of America which according to Mays and Nicholson is 42 per cent; but what is more significant, considerably less than half the Negro men attend, and this is below the proportion for white men.   Nevertheless the opinion of the universality of religious attitudes among Negroes, as contrasted to whites, persists.

It would seem that Herskovits' observation that "in an age of skepticism, the Negro has held fast to belief" requires some modification.

It may be contended that the Negro holds fast to his belief (presumably is constrained by his heritage to cling to his belief) whether or not he is a church member.   This contention is subject to question.   Indeed, results of this study, and particularly suggestions in the testimonies of cult members, warrant more than a faint suspicion that many Negroes who find their experience in the more orthodox evangelical churches a disappointment move into the cults.   It does not seem too great an assumption to imagine that for the remainder of those disappointed communicants who leave the more orthodox churches but do *not* enter the cults, many drop their belief altogether (for most practical purposes, that is, since relatively few people actually become out-and-out atheists) as well as their membership.

Hence, to the extent that Parks' suggestion of "temperament" and Herskovits' analogous use of the term "bent" imply an almost instinctive participation by American Negroes in religious pursuits, these opinions need to be received with considerable caution.

[3] Mays and Nicholson, *op. cit.*, p. 201, based on U. S. Government religious census of 1926.

THE NEGRO CHURCH AS AN AMERICAN INSTITUTION

There can be no doubt, of course, that the church, and consequently to a degree religion, have played conspicuous rôles in the lives of a vast majority of American Negroes, today and in the past. This degree of influence does not find its exact counterpart in the white man's religious experience.

As far as the Negro is concerned, Mays and Nicholson properly have pointed out that

. . . relatively early the church, and particularly the independent Negro church, furnished the one and only organized field in which the slaves' suppressed emotions could be released, and the only opportunity for him to develop his own leadership. In almost every other area he was completely suppressed. . . . Thus, through a slow and difficult process, often involving much suffering and persecution, the Negro, more than three quarters of a century prior to emancipation, through initiative, zeal and ability, began to achieve the right to be free in his church. He demonstrated his ability to preach; and this demonstration convinced both Negroes and whites that he was possessed of the Spirit of God. . . .[4]

The point to be noted is that the development of the Negro's church came as a result of the Negro's need in America for a place to express himself in various ways; it did not result from some inexorable law peculiar to his nature; neither did such a law, or as Herskovits expresses it, a "drive," constrain the Negro then or later "to turn to religion rather than to political action or other outlets for his frustration."

The two "nationalist" cults in this study are the clues in a consideration of Herskovits' assumption. What kind of people struggle politically? Obviously people who have certain political concepts. Such concepts, to result in action, cannot be divorced from life, but like the religion of the Negro according to Herskovits' characterization, it must bear an "intimate relation to life," involving the "full participation of the communicants."

Stated in political terms, in order for a people to act politically there must be political concepts, and these concepts must be made concrete by means of a political organ or organism, such as a political organization (party) or a political identity (nation). Political struggles of a national group inevitably involve that group's national identity. The struggle then becomes one in terms of that national identity, national homeland, or national unity.

[4] Mays and Nicholson, *op. cit.*, p. 3.

It is just this quality of national identity which until very recently has been lacking in the psychology of the Negroes in America. Perhaps every other sizable group in America does have such a national identity, but because of the historical factors involved in the transfer of the Negro people from Africa to America, and possibly because of the infiltration of blood from practically all the other groups in America into the veins of the Negro group, with a corresponding confusion of national emphases, the Negroes in the United States have not been conscious of those national roots which are so marked in the thinking and traditions of such elements in the American nation as the Germans, Poles, or Irish.

The Black Jews and the Moorish Americans understand some of this. The Black Jews would remind American Negroes of their ancient name and their ancient land. "Without a national name," they say, "there can be no future for a people. Therefore you must not be called Negroes, colored, jigaboos, etc." Having sounded this political note, they are impelled by the logic of their thinking to emphasize the political aspect of their life in America, even though essentially they are a religious group.

The Moorish Americans go even farther than the Black Jews. After positing the fact that the "name" is the first prerequisite, they go so far as to claim the American continent for themselves, contending that this land is merely an extension of Africa. "For a people to amount to anything," they maintain, "it is necessary to have a name [nation] and a land." Although this assumption of the American continent as an extension of their own Africa may be nothing more nor less than a political expedient, we may assume that the words fall short of action only because the Moors do not have the means to make their beliefs real.[5]

Most American Negroes, however, have not been influenced by such convictions. Consequently they have lacked strong political motivation. For such as these, Africa has not been their land, since they were uprooted spiritually as well as physically. They were not bothered by the names attached to them; if they were called Negro, colored, Afro-American, black, it was all pretty much the same thing. But neither has America been their land, since it was all too obvious to them that they were merely second-rate citizens. Inevitably in the past these great masses of Negroes have been relatively inert politically.

[5] See p. 11, note 22.

In recent years, however, there has been developing, more and more, the conviction among the masses of Negroes that America *is* their land. Today many Negroes point with pride to the fact that not even the Pilgrims may claim priority to them as settlers in the land.[6] Impressed by the increasing strength of their numbers, and beginning to appreciate the potential position of power which inheres in being the largest so-called minority group in the country, the conviction is growing among the masses of Negroes that they, as well as the Italians, Poles, Jews, Germans, and any other national groups in America, are Americans.[7]

Pari passu with this developing national pride, political consciousness and enormously increasing political action are manifesting themselves. It is no mere fortuitous circumstance that with the decline in the proportion of orthodox churchgoers indicated by Mays and Nicholson, there is an increase in the proportion of Negroes who are entering the trade unions, organizing by means of consumer coöperatives, economic boycotts, protest groups of various kinds, and those who are otherwise girding for political action.

This latter trend is no more the result of "temperament" or "bent" than is the association with religious attitudes which scholars so often ascribe to the Negro. Clearly it signifies that because of the exigencies of the times, affecting not only the Negro but the entire nation, the need for wholesale political action at last is being felt and understood among the masses of Negroes.

A mechanism for action would logically follow. It is only natural for such a mechanism to utilize the religious organization as one means of bringing about the desired end. What we witness here would seem to be a continuation of the very kind of adaptation of an institution to a given need against which the slaveholders hoped to safeguard themselves by forbidding Negroes to congregate even for purposes of religious worship. Consequently, it should come as no surprise to find in the cults, as Reid pointed out,[8] particularly in those like the Moors, the Black Jews, and the Father Divine Peace Mission Movement, leaders who are aware of these pressing needs and allow the sails of their religious

---

[6] The first Negro slaves arrived at Jamestown, Virginia, in 1619.

[7] Such organizations as the National Association for the Advancement of Colored People, the National Negro Congress, the International Brotherhood of Sleeping Car Porters, and movements like the Black Star movement of Marcus Garvey, are replete with historical evidences of this development of a national consciousness which has been increasing rapidly in recent years.

[8] Reid, *op. cit.*, p. 85.

barks to be trimmed accordingly.   Thus the Negro church maintains its American tradition.

THE AFRICAN HERITAGE

Common sense requires us to believe that everything cultural
which the Negro brought over with him from Africa could not
have been eradicated from his heritage, despite the centuries since
he left Africa, the thousands of miles which have separated him
from the ancestral homeland, and the eroding influences of an
overwhelming and inescapable super-culture.[9]   Nevertheless, if
we do not go all the way with Frazier and Park in their almost
wholesale assertions that there are no African religious survivals
to speak of, neither can we accept every chance correspondence
which might appear to indicate survival.[10]   Certainly for the
United States, where the European influence in both form and
content of the worship is so marked as to be undeniable, we are
not inclined to accept mere correspondence between American
Negro and African practice as conclusive indication of African
origin.   The historical evidence must be present to support these
clues, or so it appears to me, and much of what we observe in the
cults studied here seems to confirm this position.

Thus it is a question whether Herskovits is correct in emphasizing the importance of the influence of the African river cults
in the religious development of the American Negro.   According
to him, Negroes flocked to the Baptist church because this form
of worship was so readily associated in the minds of the Negroes
with their own river cults in West Africa, and "particularly in
view of the fact . . . that river-cult priests were sold into slavery
in great numbers." [11]   Were this the deciding factor, it seems to

[9] Herskovits has recorded the following evidences (as he believes) of African
influence on Negro ritual in North and South America: (1) spirit possession; (2)
dancing with African steps and identical motor behavior; (3) singing that derives
in manner, if not in actual form, directly from Africa; (4) references to crossing
the River Jordan (which he relates to African river-crossing); (5) wakes; (6) shal-
low burials; (7) passing of small children over coffin; (8) inclusion of food and
money in coffin; (9) fear of cursing; (10) improvisation of songs of ridicule.   See
Melville J. Herskovits, "Provenience of New World Negroes," *Social Forces*, XII
(1933), 247–62.

[10] Probably the most thorough, and certainly the most painstaking, treatment
of most of the instances of correspondence is recorded in Herskovits' most recent
work, *The Myth of the Negro Past*.   For the author's bold spirit of scientific inquiry and his careful statement and elucidation of the facts, there can be nothing
but the highest praise and deepest appreciation, although there are certain infer-
ences and conclusions by the author which we are compelled to treat with reserve.

[11] Melville J. Herskovits, "Social History of the Negro," *Handbook of Social
Psychology*, 1935, pp. 256–57.

me there should be fewer Negroes in the Methodist groups, and probably none in the other denominations which have reduced the baptismal flow to a mere trickle through the fingers. What is to be said of the Father Divine cult, with its thousands of followers who do not practise baptism? We should recall the fact that Father Divine himself probably spent his youth in that part of the South and among the very Negroes of that section who normally would be expected to cling to the most primitive attitudes regarding a ritual which was once so important and of such great significance. Besides, there are the Moorish Americans, another group of Negroes whose southern origins might be expected to result in a conservation of this ritual, but to whom the idea has become almost foreign in their Moslem form of worship.

It probably is true, as Herskovits indicates, that the elaborateness of the death ceremonies among some Negroes is an African survival. Yet in at least three of the cults studied we find that the entire association with the idea of death offers radical departures from well-known West African attitudes and practices.

The Moorish Americans maintain the same calm reserve in the presence of death which we have observed with regard to the most ordinary and simple questions of their faith. They regard death merely as a transition in which the body quietly dissolves in order to make way for the departure of the soul to Allah. Usually the body is held for three days, then there is a simple service at which a prescribed chapter of the *Holy Koran* is read, after which burial takes place. Sometimes after the burial there is a feast to celebrate the transition of the spirit from this world to the abode of Allah.

The Black Jews take death in their stride. As soon as a member of the flock dies, the body is required to be taken immediately to an undertaker's establishment. The family of the deceased goes into seclusion until after the burial. Meantime all members except very close relatives and perhaps some person designated by the prophet are forbidden to view the remains. The body is to be disposed of as soon as possible.

In the Father Divine cult, it is actually a disgrace to die. Death carries with it the penalty of being charged with having failed to fulfill the requirements of the evangelical life. The dead person becomes an outcast. It has been reported that the potter's field has become the resting place of some members of the Father Divine cult, for the simple reason that no relative or near one would claim the body of the deceased whose unfaithful living habits had required the intervention of the death angel.

None of these attitudes towards death discloses that fear of consequences so characteristic of certain West African tribes, who believe that to permit the soul of the departed to roam at large as a result of improper burial rites is certain to invite misfortunes on living members of the family of the departed one.

Even the tendency of the cults to manifest a disproportionate leader emphasis, which Herskovits has noted as an African phenomenon, does not appear to be prima facie evidence of African influence. Mary Baker Eddy, Joseph Smith, and Ann Lee are only a few leaders of predominately white religious groups in America whose preëminent place in the regard of their adherents is the same as that of the Negro cults.

"Are Negro 'shouts' due to the exposure of Negroes to the white revivalist movement?" asks Herskovits. "Or is white revivalism a reflex of those Africanisms in Negro behaviour which, in a particular kind of social setting, take the form of hysteria?" [12] He probably is the first scholar to suggest that it was the African influence on American Negro worship which conditioned the southern white camp-meeting, instead of the other way round, as numerous former students of the problem have expressed it.

In a study of northern cults there is no means of determining in what way, if any, the relation between southern white and Negro practice developed; therefore confirmation or refutation of Herskovits' position cannot be indicated here. Still, the absence of various indications of African influence which have been noted in northern cult worship, including even music in the case of the Moors, does warrant our holding in reserve the opinion which Herskovits advances. His answer to the problem is a novel and extremely interesting one, but undoubtedly a great deal more evidence than he is able to present must be adduced before his theory can be accepted.

By way of conclusion to a very interesting series of questions which arise whenever we are dealing with this matter of African survivals, I am constrained to cite two performances of religious worship which I observed recently in New York City. If there is any moral, the reader must gather it from the performances themselves:

One evening on Lenox Avenue I heard the noise of singing and shouting emanating from a second-floor hall. I mounted

[12] Herskovits, *Myth of the Negro Past*, p. 225.

the steps and entered the place, which was called Mother Horn's Pentecostal Church.

An altar service was in progress. A number of women, most of them clad in flowing white robes, were swaying before an improvised altar. Presumably these were angels, for they were praying for and administering admonitions to certain unsaved men and women who were in varying stages of prostration, some of them having fallen on one or both knees to the floor, or, in the case of a few, lying prostrate like persons in a cataleptic trance.

There was much moaning and groaning and weeping by the unsaved, accompanied by quotations from the Scriptures, shouts, admonitions, speaking in tongues, and what in some instances appeared to be exorcising, by the white-clad angels.

But the significant fact in all this performance was that of all the members who were participating the most vociferous was the minister, conspicuous by his incessant yelling from the platform; and no one was more involved in the peculiar rites of administration to the prostrate sinners than a certain woman who, I learned later, was a leader in this particular sect. But both of these leaders were members of the white race, while most of the other participants were Negroes.

There was one male devotee who approached me and spent a good part of the evening endeavoring to save my soul, alternately clapping his hands rhythmically, genuflecting, and dancing to the music which was being sung and played constantly, calling out in strange tongues, and assuring me over and over that never in all his life had he entered into such profound happiness as now since he had found his Lord and Savior. That man undoubtedly was a full-blooded American Indian.

*　*　*

On another occasion I attended a Father Divine service in Rockland Palace when a group of young Columbia University students entered the place and were seated on the platform. They had come to observe Father Divine at first hand.

It was easy to see in their faces that many of them fully anticipated an evening's entertainment consonant with popular ideas of African fetish or Haitian voodoo worship.

A very quizzical look spread over the countenances of some of these when, quite early in the service, an elderly white man arose and walked to the platform, stood by the microphone, and called out to the vast audience, consisting chiefly of Negroes, "Peace, Father! Peace, everyone!"

Thereupon he praised Father Divine for his many blessings, and especially for one blessing above all others, namely, the blessing of life everlasting. He turned to the Columbia students and said to them, "I know that you may not believe this, but many of us who are in this place will never lose the bodies we now have. God is here in the flesh, and he is never going away from us, and we will remain here forevermore. This is heaven on earth."

Now he asked everyone to join with him in a song which he said was familiar to audiences in the West, but was relatively unknown to followers of Father Divine in the East. The words of the song were as follows:

> My Father's love shines more and more.
> My Father's love shines more and more.
> Oh, glory hallelujah! Praise his holy name!
> For his love shines more and more.

In a few seconds his song had caught on all over the huge amphitheatre. And then an amazing spectacle followed:

A white woman who had been playing castanets in the Father Divine Peace Mission orchestra suddenly leaped to her feet and began dancing back and forth across the front of the hall.

The white cornetist, who for a while played in the manner of Louis Armstrong, was so profoundly affected that he had to cease playing, and he joined lustily in the singing, shaking his head and his entire body in rhythm with the song. Presumably playing the cornet interfered with the execution of the body movements he was desirous of performing.

Then another white woman circled conspicuously in pinwheel fashion all over the front of the hall, while a very heavy-set, middle-aged man, whom I later identified as a Jew, ran about the same place clapping his hands rhythmically, singing loudly and gaily, and contorting his face and body.

Still another white follower, a well-clad young man seated on the platform, kept moving his body forward in his chair, then backward, in time with the music. And finally, one of the Columbia University students, too overcome to remember where she was or what she was doing, began to sing freely and to tap the floor with her feet.

This spectacle which the Columbia students had expected to see generated by Negroes, had been inspired by an elderly white man from California, Scandinavian by race and accent, and had been brought to a high crescendo pitch largely through the reactions of white members of the cult. The spell was so tremendous that, even after the music had ceased, the former castanet player continued to race around in circles in front of the hall, while the gentleman of estwhile Jewish faith indulged in an orgy of jumping about, puffing, blowing, perspiring, clapping his hands, and flapping his arms in imitation of angels' wings. Here for all the world to hear and see, they proclaimed, Father Divine is God!

XI

SUMMARY OF FINDINGS

THE data in this study, while admittedly limited, offer the following indications:

1. It is a fair inference that the apparent over-emphasis by the American Negro in the religious sphere is related to the comparatively meager participation of Negroes in other institutional forms of American culture, such as business, politics, and industry, a condition which is bound up intimately with the prevailing custom of racial dichotomy which restricts the normal participation of Negroes in many avenues of American life. On the other hand, the study does not present adequate grounds for believing that there is an instinctive religious "bent" or "temperament" which sets apart the American Negro from other Americans in his quest for the satisfaction of basic urges or needs through religious processes.

2. Because the American Negro's experience in other institutional or "secular" forms is limited, the one institution with which he is closely identified tends to act as a channel for various kinds of expression. Thus the Negro leader finds in the church a mechanism preëminently suited to the needs of leadership along numerous lines. It seems reasonable to suppose that many of these leadership expressions would not develop within the framework of the religious experience of the Negro if the outlets for expression in other institutionalized life in our culture were more normal.

3. Negroes are attracted to the cults for the obvious reason that with few normal outlets of expression for Negroes in America due to the prevailing custom of racial dichotomy the cults offer on the one hand the boon of religion with all its attendant promise of heaven either here or above or both; and on the other hand they provide for certain Negroes with imagination and other dynamic qualities, in an atmosphere free from embarrassment or apology, a place where they may experiment in activities such as business, politics, social reform, and social expression; thereby these American Negroes satisfy the normal urge of any member

of our culture who wishes to contribute positively to the advancement of the group.

4. The personality of the leader of the cult frequently is a very substantial determining factor in the attractiveness of the particular cult to its members.

5. The American Negro religious cult exercises rigid taboos over certain features of the private lives of its members, frequently reaching into the most intimate details of their lives. Sex inhibitions are of paramount importance in most of the cult groups.

6. American Negro religious cults practise forms of endogamy, in some instances proscribing even with regard to race. But in the Father Divine cult, where marriage is strictly forbidden, there is much greater social catholicity within the cult.

7. Singing, dancing, shouting, clapping the hands, etc., while generally characteristic of American Negro cult worship, are not essential features. The Moors definitely contradict such an assumption.

8. There is much greater use of the place of worship for religious purposes by the American Negro cult than by the more orthodox evangelical churches.

9. There is an indication that as American Negro cults become more intent upon social, economic, and political problems, the literal adherence to the Bible as a book of reference diminishes. The most rigid adherence to the Bible is by the cults which have the least notable political or economic programs, and conversely, those cults with original economic, social, and political programs tend to develop their own sets of rules, even going so far as to discard the Bible almost entirely.

10. The theory that Negroes in the United States demonstrate survival characteristics of African influence in the form, ritual, and spirit of their religious worship must be received with considerable caution. That there is a modicum of such influence undoubtedly is true, but this is overwhelmingly outweighed by American cultural influences.

As a concluding observation, we surmise from these evidences, with other general observations of the American Negro's religious life, that the Negro church is still to be reckoned with as a positive factor in the further social, political, and economic development of the American Negro. But it would be wrong, we believe, to interpret this conclusion as a substantiation of Herskovits' impression that the Negro religious "bent" impels him to "turn to religion rather than to political action or other outlets for his frustration." [1]

Because of historic reasons, obviously the American Negro church will continue to act as an important social mechanism for Negro leadership and for the masses. But for the very reason that Negro leaders still find it necessary to have recourse to the church mechanism (bearing in mind, however, that other mechanisms such as the trade union, coöperatives, etc., now appear on the threshold) it is also clear, as the evidence of some of the cults indicates, that the American Negro church is likely to witness a transformation from its purely religious function to functions which will accommodate the urgent social needs of the Negro masses under modern stresses of politics and economics. Is it fantastic to imagine that, as time passes, the American Negro church may bear a relationship to the original religious institution of our memory somewhat analogous to the relationship which the modern drug store bears to the nineteenth century apothecary shop?

The earlier quoted observation of Ira De A. Reid with regard to the cults in particular is very pertinent in this connection. The discernible response of these cults to certain dynamic urges which motivate the American Negro's present-day psychology undoubtedly has more than passing significance. The original revolutionary potential of the American Negro church may again be in evidence in these phenomena. Thus a Negro Baptist clergyman has utilized the religious mechanism in order to have himself elected to the council chambers of New York City, another one to the legislative halls of Pennsylvania. The activities of Father Divine in the political and economic fields, to use a notable example among the cults, are suggestive evidences of the continuing dynamic character of the American Negro's religious experience in a milieu which has made the unique unfolding of that experience compulsory and inevitable.

[1] Cf. Herskovits, *The Myth of the Negro Past.*

Appendix A

SELECTED CASE MATERIALS

THESE examples of testimonies and case histories have been selected from the mass of data collected during the course of the study because they seem typical of the entire collection. Limitation of space due to war restrictions on the use of paper has made it necessary to eliminate all but a few representative samples.

* * *

H. C. is a young man, age about thirty. When he was considerably younger and had finished high school in Philadelphia he wanted to go to college. He had a hard time of it, what with sickness and financial difficulties. He was pretty far down in the dumps. He had been attending the Baptist church and was anxious to get help through the church, but there was no help forthcoming to relieve his mind. His sister-in-law was a member of Mt. Olive Holiness Church. All the time she talked to him about Mt. Sinai. He commenced going there. At first it was difficult for him,. but the elders assured him that if he persevered and had faith he would come through all right. He was very sincere and earnest about all this. He tried to have a vision. He had difficulty in speaking in tongues, but they taught him to say "Jesus, Jesus, Jesus," very fast, and he kept doing that so much that one day he found himself automatically speaking in tongues and leaping and shouting and rejoicing. He thought Elder Jeffries was just the most wonderful person in the world. He had complete faith in her and in her wisdom. She was a woman of God. One day he had a frightful pain over his heart, just the kind of pain that previously had put him to bed for several weeks at a stretch. He told Elder Jeffries about it. She put her hand on him. Instantly the pain left him and he was completely healed. Since then H. C. received his college education, but in the meantime he lost his belief and zeal in the Mt. Sinai church.

* * *

Mrs. F.: "I am glad to speak a few words for Daddy Grace, and tell what he means to me. I was sick for many years; I was treated by different doctors, and they gave me all kinds of medicine in vain. So, in September 1933, Elder C. B. Williams came from Greenville, South Carolina, and opened a mission and held night services. He told us about the House of Prayer and Daddy Grace. He preached so many good things about Daddy Grace that he made me see the light that

111

Daddy is the Savior. I joined the mission, and through the power of the Savior I was healed. While we held services in the mission I worked hard as secretary. It came to pass that we had no place to worship. In 1936, during Daddy's tenth anniversary in Charlotte, North Carolina, I asked him to build for us. And he said, 'You shall have it.' Soon after that he sent Elder E. Hall to build for us. After he had finished the building, Daddy made his first visit to us in person on that occasion. He asked Elder Hall, 'Didn't I come to you when you were asleep and told you how to build this house?' And Elder Hall answered, 'Yes sir, Daddy.' And too I want to say that there is healing power in the *Grace Magazine*, and the products is my doctor. I use them for medicine, and I be healed both soul and body. Thank God for that, and for Daddy Grace, for he is the cause of it all. He caused me to live holy. Pray for me."

* * *

Mrs. M. G.: "I wish to testify of the wonderful healing power which is in the *Grace Magazine*. I am not a member of the House of Prayer, but Elder Bush was the one that gave me the *Grace Magazine*. I suffered a long time with a pain in my side. The *Grace Magazine* was the only thing that healed me. Pray for me that I will soon have more faith and be a member of the House of Prayer."

* * *

Mrs. R. W.: "For five years I suffered with the agonizing pains of the rheumatism. I tried different remedies but they did not help me. At last when all hopes were gone, Elder Bush, a minister of the House of Prayer, gave me a magazine and I applied it to my body and I was healed. I am not a member but I thank God for such a wonderful prayer. Pray for me that I will become a member."

* * *

Daddy Grace: "The only provision for salvation is by Grace. Never mind about God. Salvation is by Grace only. Ephesians 2:8. You must come to Grace through faith. The great trouble with the world today is that people are worshipping God in heaven and still hate Grace and will not hear his words. God and Grace are one. God is invisible and Grace is visible. God is the background of Grace. Whenever Grace appears on earth, God is present but unseen. Grace to us is God in the sense of salvation. The only prayer that is to be prayed now is, Lord give us Grace. The great trouble today is that the people are pretentiously worshipping God in heaven and at the same time they will not hear His word. It is impossible to worship God acceptably and hate His word. Grace has given God a vacation, and since God is on His vacation, don't worry Him. Bring all your troubles and all your worries to the throne of Grace and they will be taken care of. But instead of doing that the people ignore Grace and say all manner of evil against him and still pray to God. But remember, if you sin against God, Grace can save you, but if you sin against Grace, God cannot save you. God made His man and sent him to the people that they may follow him. God is a Creator, and not a leader of people. God made the earth for man, and He ordains a man to lead the people the way that He would have them to go, which is the only right way."

* * *

D. L. is a concrete worker and cement mixer. He loves business. He was born in Montgomery County, Georgia, and as a boy helped his father on the farm. His father was quite well-to-do at one time and it was nothing for him to bale eighty bales of cotton in one year. His father owned several plots of land, altogether about four hundred acres. Consequently D. L. was reared in business because he had to attend to the sale of his father's cotton, buying and selling land and equipment for the farms. But he practically never went to school. He works hard for a living, but he believes that God does not intend for man to work in the winter time when there is bad weather. If you read Deuteronomy, Exodus, and Leviticus you can see how God intends for man to farm, and how he should harvest, when he should stop work. Also it is very clear from the Bible that women should remain at home and bear children. At the age of twenty-one, D. L. left his father and came North. He liked church and got into all kinds of religions. Finally he became a preacher under ————. He had the Philadelphia district. But when ———— got into some trouble over a girl, he wanted D. L. to take the rap for it even though he was a married man. His wife heard ———— order him to take the rap, and she would not let him do it. He split from ———— and came into Prophet Cherry's church. The thing he likes about Prophet Cherry is that he teaches Negroes to be independent, to go into business for themselves, and not to call themselves Negroes. He believes that Negroes ought to keep to themselves and not mix up at all with whites. Every boy should get a trade. He believes that there should be music and dancing in the church because during the forty years the children of Israel were in the wilderness they danced. He has been in a number of businesses since being in Philadelphia. He opened up a shoe-repair shop in 1934 with only six dollars. Three dollars he used for the rent of a shop, and the other three he paid down on some repairing machines. He developed three such shops, employing a number of colored men. He also ran a bus for transportation (used his own big automobile) and had a grocery store. But he had to close all but one of his shoe-repair shops because his help proved incompetent and unreliable. He believes that all the saints were black men; that white people never came into the church until after Jesus; that Jacob was black but Esau was white; that when Esau married some black folk, we got the yellow folk.

* * *

W. G. despises gentiles (i. e., whites). He despises Negroes also who insist on acting like, behaving like, thinking like, and being like gentiles. W. G. calls white Jews orthodox Jews. He extols the virtues of his own cult, especially the way in which the members interest themselves in the welfare of any stricken member. W. G. labeled a Negro "Paul" because this Negro scoffs at Prophet Cherry's teachings and attempts to make a case for gentiles. W. G. is sure that the sun is the biggest star because the Bible contains a verse which says no star is bigger than the sun and the sun is ten thousand times as strong as the strongest star. W. G. is bitter against preachers. He says they know nothing. They exploit the people. He does not attend motion pictures, does not smoke. Drinking is all right, he says, and he will quote the Scriptures to prove that God intended that man should use intoxicating beverages. But it is a sin to get drunk. All church services, he says, should be orderly. There ought to be a moderation of shouting and crying out, but members may dance if they wish provided they do not have mixed dancing, which is a sin and an abomination. W. G. believes there are three heavens: the heaven of the birds, the aeroplane, and the stars. Recently W. G. brought his mother and father to Philadelphia. They have since joined Prophet Cherry's synagogue.

* * *

Letter from a parent who is a member of Prophet Cherry's cult (Black Jews) to a teacher in the public schools regarding patriotism, etc.[1]

Dear ————

W———— was telling me that he would not salute the American flag this morning when he was told. I don't want him to be rude to you or disobedient in all things that are right, but the flag is not our flag and there is a likeness of an eagle on the top of the flag pole and this is not right in the sight of God. Therefore we do not care to salute the flag. This is not our country. We are not free here. If we were, there would be no segregation. We are the only nation of people in this country that is segregated because of our color and nationality. I still remember how Mr. ———— and some of our school teachers were treated in Harrisburg at some restaurant where they wanted to sit down and eat like other civilized and intelligent people. If our best people are treated in this manner simply because they wanted food to eat, just food that's all, what about the poor common class of us like myself? Think of it. All this and many other more

---

[1] This letter was written before Pearl Harbor.

inhuman things that happens to us in this country proves to me that we are not free citizens of this country. We were brought over here in 1619 as slaves to work for this nation that rules this country and we served 245 years and we are now only part free by the will of God not Abe Lincoln, for God can use anything that he made. Give God the praise, not man. We were chased out of Palestine by the Romans (Italian) into the west coast of Africa where we were captured and sold into this great U. S. A. God said we must return to our homeland at a set time. Read Deut. 28 chapter, see the reason why we were made slaves. Ex. 20 chapter, why we do not bow to idol gods such as the eagle on the flag. Amos 9th chapter tells of our return home after the Battle of Armageddon which will be in Palestine. There is so much in the Bible that tells us about us that is the only sure and correct history concerning us and all the other nations.

Now M————, I only wrote this to you that you might understand why we refuse to do some things that the ruling nations require. Not to break our friendship as teacher and parent and child, but to bring us closer together. These things are not taught to us in schools and colleges and seminaries because the other nations want to keep us in ignorance of our beginning. God said we are his chosen people and that we are a royal people. We should love God first and love the nations too, but His law comes first. Therefore we are like Daniel and the three Hebrew boys in the days of old (They are our people too). We are not careful to follow the laws and rules of the heathen nations when they are against God's laws. . . . I would that all of my people knew what a great and royal nation we are and stop believing everything the other nations put on us. Thank you.

Yours truly,

———— ————

* * *

Notes from colloquy between a member of the Moorish Science Temple and interviewer. The letters "M" and "I" represent the cult member and interviewer respectively.

I: "What is your religious denomination?"

M: (Somewhat shocked by the question) "The only great one, sir, the only real one, sir. Mohammedan. There's only one God, sir, the great God, Allah. I am a Moorish American, sir."

I: "What is your nationality?"

M: "American, sir. Because I was born in America, but *my* ancestors were *great* Asiatic peoples, Moors, with a free national country. We're Moorish Americans." M then bent close to his questioner and asked, "And now, young man, what are *you?* Every free people have a national country with a flag. Just ask a German born in this country and he'll quickly tell you 'German' and that his foreparents came from Germany. Now what are you?"

I: "You are looking at me. Suppose you tell me what I am."

M: (After some deliberation) "A Negro? What's a Negro? Nothing but a name of contempt and scorn placed on a free national people to make them slaves. Black? Ethiopian? Both the same thing. Nothing but names used by the palefaces to oppress a free national people. . . . Why, the so-called 'Negro' has no nation, no flag to claim. The same is true of the so-called 'blacks' and 'Ethiopians.' No such thing as Negro, black, Ethiopian." Then in a tone of warning: "The time is coming soon when all free people will have to know their nationality. So what are you?"

I: "Suppose I told you I am an American?"

M: (With a decided chuckle) "American what? Paleface? Just tell one of them that and see!" (More chuckling) "Your skin and hair look very much like my folks."

I: "What is the meaning of the term 'bey' at the end of your name?"

M: "What my people once were, sir—great rulers. You know, of course, who the first rulers of this country were?" He said this with evident pride, head proudly erect.

I: "You mean the Indians?"

M: "That's what they told you in school, but that's wrong. The great Asiatics were the first to rule this country. My people. And I can get you plenty of proof, because the palefaces dare not tell you the truth. But my folks know better." M continued passionately: "The palefaces have made beggars out of all my people. For one hundred and fifty years my people were kept in darkness and worked like beasts to build this country and then were turned loose with nothing, to be beggars. We want decent things for ourselves. We want to do the right thing by our children. We want to educate them, even to send them to college. But what do we have to do it with? Nothing! Beggars! That's all we are. . . . All before 1935, I lived in darkness. In ignorance. But now I know. My people are a great people, a free national people. We're from a great country. All free people have a national country." And then a final word before departing: "And now, my friend, between me and you, what are you? After all, it's time that you knew!"

* * *

XYZ: "I was studying for the ministry. But I became more and more dissatisfied with Christianity, especially its hypocrisy, where we Negroes are concerned. Finally I decided I could not stand it. Then a man from India spoke to me about Mohammed. I liked everything I heard, and the more I read the more I liked it. They told me I did not have to join but if I wished I was welcome. Now I am a leader and a teacher."

* * *

Four women in a Father Divine Peace Mission dress shop: Three of these were about fifty years of age, and the fourth a younger woman, about thirty-five. All but one had come from outside New York City, one from the South, another from Kansas, and the third from Cincinnati. The interviewer entered the shop about 10:30 one summer evening, when all four were working over sewing machines or with scissors. When the interviewer asked them if they would mind enlightening him a bit about the Father Divine movement, one of the older women said she doubted that anything she could say would help him because each person had to get his understanding of the Father in his own way. The best way would be for him to read the *New Day* and attend the meetings, another said. The third one remarked, "Not any one of us got the divine revelation in the same way, and if a million people enter into the spirit, they will enter in a million different ways." They discussed among themselves the worthwhileness of talking with the interviewer. They said if he had come merely out of curiosity, it was doubtful if anything they might say would help him. Besides, they had their own understanding, but only Father and the *New Day* could speak with authority. Nothing they would say could be accounted the gospel truth.

One of the older women was more inclined to talk than any of the others. The interviewer addressed himself to her, and told her he was puzzled by a few things in the Peace Mission Movement. For example, he was unable to note any praying, and since he had come up in a church where prayer was an important part of the service, was he correct in believing that Father Divinites did not pray? She said that the interviewer was wrong. She quoted from the Bible, "Prayer is the expression of the heart's desire." She said every word that a person might utter could be a prayer. Our very breathing is a prayer. Especially everything about us that causes us to be grateful is a prayer. The fact is that the followers of Father Divine do not pray in the way others do because prayer assumes that God is far off somewhere and you have to petition him. But God is here with us (Father Divine). It no longer is necessary to send a petition to him. He is in our midst, sees us and knows us. And that is why, instead of praying in the usual way, they say over and over, "Thank you, Father!" The youngest woman then spoke up. She said yes, that prayer is on their lips constantly, and it makes them very happy. When she goes to bed she can feel that prayer beating within her. When she turns in her bed, her very muscles and tissues say, "Thank you, Father," and it makes her very happy.

The interviewer asked them about baptism. They told him that baptism in the old sense has been done away with. Water baptism was a form. Now we are baptized in the spirit. They told him it is like cotton; when you plant the seed, you say you are planting cotton; when it begins to shoot up, you say you must tend the cotton;

when you find it in full bloom, you say you must pick the cotton; then you say you must seed it.   Yet all the while you are not talking about the cotton at all.   Only the final product is the cotton, and only that is useful.   All the rest is useless and worse than useless, because if it gets mixed in with the final product it will spoil it.   So it is with baptism with water.   All these things lead up to the spiritual life, but they are not the spiritual life.   Once this life is attained, all these other things are useless and could even be harmful.   Father Divine has come to do away with all harmful things.

The interviewer asked if it were true that most of Father Divine's followers once had been very wayward children.   This question stirred considerable resentment.   The women as much as told him that his question was insulting.   If anyone would look, they said, he would see for himself.   The interviewer had been present at various meetings.   Did it appear to him that most of the followers belonged to the scum of the earth?   Did they seem to be bums and criminals?   One of the older women said she had grown up in a fine home, with splendid surroundings and background.   In certain respects there were things in her home which were not provided for in Father's life.   But she had forsaken these in order to live a life of evangelical faith.

All these women protested that they had not come to Father Divine because of a sense of dereliction, but because they felt his call.   The youngest woman said she had begun to find the call more than four years ago in Cincinnati.   She kept asking herself, "Can Father Divine be God?"   She went to her room and prayed constantly to God to let her know whether or not Father Divine was God.   None of her immediate family was a follower.   One morning, about three o'clock, a voice spoke out to her.   It said, "I am God, and you will find me in the body of Father Divine.   Have no fear; you will be saved."   It was a most thrilling moment for her, she said.   She could hardly wait for morning to come.   When finally it had arrived, she went downstairs and told other members of her family.   They laughed at her and derided her.   She went over to the local Peace Mission.   There she found sympathy and comfort.   Within four months the call to be near the presence of God was so strong that she left Cincinnati and came to New York City, where she has been ever since.   She is so glad she let the bit be placed in her mouth!

One of the older women said she had had a very good home with fine surroundings as a girl, but that she had been very petulant, obstinate, willful, and ungrateful for everything she received from her loving parents.   She constantly found fault, picked quarrels, and the like.   Then she came under the influence of Father Divine's teachings.   Her entire nature has changed.   She lives a life of complete happiness.   She never finds fault.   She never argues or gets into quarrels.   Life is a happy song.   She loves her work; thinks nothing of beginning very early in the morning and finishing at five o'clock the next morning. In fact, she said, and her friends said the same for themselves, sometimes she was not altogether glad to go to sleep; life was so beautiful and wonderful. They spoke of the Rosebuds' singing. These songs are inspirations of Father. He will put a song on your lips and when you utter it, everyone will join in. Some of the Rosebuds are children of the followers, and others have come right off the streets. They live pure, evangelical lives, and are devoted to Father. There are more than one hundred of these alone. Also there are Crusaders among the boys. These refute the claim that all the followers of Father Divine are old people. They told me that followers of Father Divine do not use the term "Heaven" when referring to one of his hostels. This is a derisive term used by outsiders. Actually there is a heaven for every individual, and that heaven is within. Only that. Color is completely out with Father Divine's followers. Father Divine himself has no color. He is the expression of everybody and everything.

TABLE I
ORGANIZATION OF CULTS

Cults	Religious Faith	Metropolitan Centers	Location in Phila.
Mt. Sinai Holy Church	Christian (Holiness)	Philadelphia	Oxford St., west of 21st
United House of Prayer	Christian (Holiness)	Washington	16th St., below Fitzwater
Church of God	Modified Judaism	Philadelphia	2132 Nicholas St.
Moorish Science Temple	Moslem	Chicago	Christian St. at 18th[a]
Father Divine Peace Mission Movement	Christian Eclectic	Philadelphia[b]	Broad and Catherine sts.

Founders	Sacred Book	Role of Leader	Segregation of Sexes
Bishop Ida Robinson	Bible	Ordained by God	No
Bishop C. M. Grace	Bible	Co-equal with Jesus	No
Prophet F. S. Cherry	Talmud	Called personally by God	No[d]
Prophet Noble Drew Ali	Holy Koran of Noble Drew Ali	Mohammed reincarnated	Yes
Father Divine	New Day[c]	God	Yes

[a] At the time of this study, the Moorish Temple was located on Lombard St., between 15th and 16th.
[b] At the time of this study, Father Divine's headquarters were in New York City.
[c] The Bible is consulted also.
[d] Fairly strict.

Table II

Functional Developments of Cults

	Racial Emphasis	Schools for Instruction	Business Establish- ments	Retreats	Special Texts	Pol. & Econ. Programs
Mt. Sinai Holy Church....	—	X	X	X	—	—
United House of Prayer...	—	—	—	—	—	—
Church of God..........	X	X	X	—	X[c]	—
Moorish Science Temple...	X	X	X	—	X	X
Peace Mission Movement..	X[a]	X[b]	X	X	X	X

[a] Emphasis on absence of racial distinction.

[b] In addition to schools within the cult, all services are in the nature of special instruction.

[c] Talmud.

Table III

Factors Which Attract Communicants to the Cult
(in order of importance)

1. Personality of leader.
1. Desire to get closer to God.
3. Racial or nationalistic urge.
4. Miraculous cure.
5. Dissatisfaction with Christianity.
6. Disdain of orthodox church.
7. Mental relief.
8. Urge for leadership and participation.
9. Aid to business.
10. Disdain of ministers.
11. Instruction within the cult.
12. Common bond of friendliness and understanding.

Table IV[a]

Negro Church Denominations in Philadelphia

	Number	Percentage
Baptists.........................	112	47.6
African Methodists................	26	11.1
Holiness.........................	49	20.9
All others.......................	48	20.4

[a] From Mays and Nicholson, *The Negro's Church.*

BIBLIOGRAPHY

ALLEN, RICHARD. *The Life of Richard Allen.* Philadelphia, 1880.

APTHEKER, HERBERT. "American Negro Slave Revolts," *Science and Society,* I (1937), 512–38.

——. *The Negro in the Civil War.* New York, 1938.

——. *Negro Slave Revolts in the United States.* New York, 1939.

BALLAGH, JAMES C. *A History of Slavery in Virginia.* Baltimore, 1902.

BASCOM, W. R. "Acculturation among the Gullah Negroes," *American Anthropologist,* XLIII (1941), 43–50.

BILLINGS, R. A. "The Negro and His Church; a Psychogenetic Study," *Psychoanalytic Review,* XXI (1934), 425–41.

BIRD, RICHARD S. "Expansion of the Father Divine Movement," *New York Times,* Section IV, July 2, 1939.

BRAGG, GEORGE FREEMAN. *History of the Afro-American Group of the Episcopal Church.* Baltimore, 1922.

COE, GEORGE A. *The Spiritual Life, Studies in the Science of Religion.* New York, 1900.

——. *The Psychology of Religion.* Chicago, 1916.

CROMWELL, JOHN W. "First Negro Churches in the District of Columbia," *Journal of Negro History,* VII (1922), 64–106.

——. "Aftermath of Nat Turner's Insurrection," *Journal of Negro History,* V (1920), 208–34.

DAVENPORT, F. M. *Primitive Traits in Religious Revivals; A Study in Mental and Social Evolution.* New York, 1905.

DAVIS, ALLISON, and DOLLARD, JOHN. *Children of Bondage.* Washington, 1940.

DOWD, JEROME. *The Negro in American Life.* New York, 1926.

DUBOIS, WILLIAM E. BURGHARDT (ed.). *Economic Coöperation among Negro Americans* (Atlanta University Publications, Volume 12). Atlanta, 1907.

——. *The Negro.* New York, 1915.

EARNEST, JOSEPH BRUMMELL. *The Religious Development of the Negro in Virginia.* Charlottesville, 1914.

ELLIS, ALFRED B. *The Tshi-speaking Peoples of the Gold Coast of West Africa.* London, 1887.

——. *The Ewe-speaking Peoples of the Slave Coast of West Africa.* London, 1890.

——. *A History of the Gold Coast of West Africa.* London, 1893.

EMBREE, E. R. *Brown America, the Story of a New Race.* New York, 1931.

FRAZIER, E. FRANKLIN. *The Negro Family in the United States.* Chicago, 1939.

——. *Negro Youth at the Crossways.* Washington, 1940.

FRY, C. LUTHER. *The United States Looks at its. Churches.* New York, 1930.

GILLARD, JOHN T. *Colored Catholics in the United States.* Baltimore, 1941.

GUILD, JUNE PURCELL. *Black Laws of Virginia.* Richmond, 1936.

HAYNES, GEORGE E. "The Church and Negro Progress," *Annals of the American Academy of Political and Social Science,* November 1928.

HERSKOVITS, MELVILLE J. "The Negro's Americanism," in Alain Locke (ed.), *The New Negro* (pp. 353–60). New York, 1925.

——. *The American Negro, a Study in Racial Crossing.* New York, 1928.

——. "The Negro in the New World; The Statement of a Problem," *American Anthropologist,* XXXII (1930), 145–55.

——. "On the Provenience of New World Negroes," *Social Forces,* XII (1933), 247–62.

——. "The Social History of the Negro," in C. Murchison (ed.), *Handbook of Social Psychology* (pp. 207–67). Worcester, Mass., 1935.

——. "What Has Africa Given America?" *The New Republic,* LXXXIV (1935), 92–94.

——. "The Significance of West Africa for Negro Research," *Journal of Negro History,* XXI (1936), 15–30.

——. "African Gods and Catholic Saints in New World Negro Belief," *American Anthropologist,* XXXIX (1937), 635–43.

——. "The Significance of the Study of Acculturation for Anthropology," *American Anthropologist,* XXXIX (1937), 259–64.

——. *Acculturation, the Study of Culture Contact.* New York, 1938.

——. *The Myth of the Negro Past.* New York, 1941.

HOSHOR, JOHN. *God in a Rolls Royce.* New York, 1936.

JAMES, WILLIAM. *The Varieties of Religious Experience.* New York, 1902.

JOHNSON, CHARLES S. *Shadow of the Plantation.* Chicago, 1934.

——. *Growing Up in the Black Belt: Negro Youth in the Rural South.* Washington, 1941.

——. *Patterns of Negro Segregation.* New York, 1943.

JOHNSON, GUY B. "The Negro Spiritual, a Problem in Anthropology," *American Anthropologist,* XXXIII (1931), 157–71.

JOHNSTON, SIR HARRY. *The Negro in the New World.* London, 1910.

JONES, CHARLES C. *The Religious Instruction of the Negroes in the United States.* Savannah, 1842.

Jones, Raymond Julius. *A Comparative Study of Religious Cult Behavior among Negroes with Special Reference to Emotional Group Conditioning Factors.* Washington, 1939.

Kirkpatrick, Clifford. *Religion in Human Affairs.* New York and London, 1929.

Levy-Bruhl, Lucien. *How Natives Think.* London, 1926.

Lips, Julius E. *The Savage Hits Back.* New Haven, 1937.

Locke, Alain (ed.). *The New Negro.* New York, 1925.

——. *The Negro and His Music.* Washington, 1926.

——, and Stern, Bernhard J. *When Peoples Meet.* New York, 1942.

Mair, Lucy Philip. *An African People in the Twentieth Century.* London, 1934.

Malinowski, B. *Argonauts of the Western Pacific.* New York, 1922.

——. *The Foundations of Faith and Morals.* London, 1936.

——. "The Group and the Individual in Functional Analysis," *American Journal of Sociology,* XLIV (1939), No. 6, 938–64.

Marett, R. R. *The Threshold of Religion.* London, 1909.

——. *Faith, Hope and Charity in Primitive Religion.* New York, 1932.

Matlack, Lucius C. *The History of American Slavery and Methodism, 1780–1849.* New York, 1849.

Mays, Benjamin Elijah, and Nicholson, Joseph William. *The Negro's Church.* New York, 1933.

Nassau, Robert H. *Fetishism in West Africa; Forty Years' Observation of Native Customs and Superstitions.* New York, 1904.

Park, Robert E. "The Conflict and Fusion of Culture," *Journal of Negro History,* IV (1919).

Parker, R. A. *The Incredible Messiah.* Boston, 1937.

Payne, Daniel Alexander. *History of the AME Church.* Nashville, 1891.

Pitt-Rivers, George Henry Lane Fox. *The Clash of Culture and the Contact of Races.* London, 1927.

Powdermaker, Hortense. *After Freedom.* New York, 1939.

Puckett, Newbell N. *Folk Beliefs of the Southern Negro.* Chapel Hill, 1926.

Rattray, R. S. *Ashanti.* Oxford, 1923.

——. *Religion and Art in Ashanti.* Oxford, 1927.

Reid, Ira De A. *In a Minor Key.* Washington, 1940.

Reuter, Edward Byron. *American Race Problem.* New York, 1938.

Starbuck, Edwin D. *Psychology of Religion.* London and New York, 1901.

Thurnwald, Richard C. *Black and White in East Africa.* London, 1935.

Warner, W. Lloyd. "Social Anthropology and the Modern Community," *American Journal of Sociology,* XLVI (1941), 785–96.

Warner, W. Lloyd, Junker, Buford H., and Adams, Walter A. *Color and Human Nature; Negro Personality Development in a Northern City.* Washington, 1941.

Weatherford, W. D. *The Negro from Africa to America.* New York, 1924.

———, and Johnson, Charles. *Race Relations; Adjustment of Whites and Negroes in the United States.* New York, 1934.

Wesley, Charles H. *Richard Allen, Apostle of Freedom.* Washington, 1935.

Wilson, G. R. "Religion of the American Negro Slave," *Journal of Negro History,* Vol. VIII (1923).

Woodson, Carter G. *The Education of the Negro Prior to 1861.* New York and London, 1915.

———. *The History of the Negro Church.* Washington, 1921.

———. *The Negro in Our History.* Washington, 1941.

Woofter, T. J. *The Economic Status of the Negro.* Chapel Hill, 1930.

———. *Negro Problems in Cities.* New York, 1928.

Work, Monroe (ed.). *Negro Year Book, 1937–38.* Tuskegee Institute.

Young, Donald. *American Minority Peoples.* New York, 1932.

ARTHUR HUFF FAUSET, a rebel by nature and by heritage, wished to be "a fighting leader." He has achieved this desire within the limits of his times, activities, and geographical foci.

His mother was white and a Christian convert of Jewish heritage; his father, black and an African Methodist Episcopal minister. Born in Flemington, New Jersey, Fauset grew up in Philadelphia. The racial and religious mixture within his family, and the tolerant perspective of his mother aided in the development of Fauset's ecumenical attitude which has guided many of his activities. As a youth, he was frequently likened to his father, who died when Fauset was an infant but left a reputation for outspoken beliefs and actions.

Fauset graduated from Central High School and the School of Pedagogy for Men in Philadelphia. Subsequently, he became a teacher, and shortly afterwards, a principal in the Philadelphia public school system. While teaching, he attended the University of Pennsylvania, and became both a student and a close friend of Frank G. Speck who directed him into anthropology. On Professor Speck's recommendation, Fauset was sponsored by Elsie Clews Parsons to do folklore research among blacks in Nova Scotia, the South and the West Indies. His master's thesis, *Folklore From Nova Scotia (American Folklore Society Memoirs, XXIV, 1931)*, the first collection of black folklore in Canada, resulted from his initial expedition.

By the 1930's, Fauset had become involved in militant civil rights activism. Alain Locke, author of *The New Negro* (New York, 1925) and other works on black culture, was his intimate friend and a strong influence in shaping his philosophy. He has also been associated with many other blacks who have gained prominence including W. E. B. Du Bois, Paul Robeson, A. Philip Randolph, Adam Clayton Powell. He served as Vice-President of the Philadelphia teacher's union which he had helped reorganize. For several years he was National Vice-President of the National Negro Congress, an organization suited to his militant bent.

Concurrently, Fauset worked on his doctorate under Speck and A. Irving Hallowell. His major concerns were, however, "things that were happening out in the street," and his involvement with anthropology was, therefore, more inquisitive than academic. His pragmatic search for relevance in education prompted his choice of dissertation subjects—the study presented in this volume was originally his doctoral dissertation for the University of Pennsylvania.

Awarded the Ph.D. in 1942, he became one of America's first black anthropologists. In spite of this, he continued to turn from academic life. He has, however, continuously maintained his membership in the American Anthropological Association of which he is a Fellow.

During World War II, he entered the army, but just before being commissioned was honorably discharged because of his prior civil rights activities. Fauset then organized, and until 1946 served as Chairman of, the United People's Action Committee in Philadelphia. At the same time, he edited the Philadelphia edition of Adam Clayton Powell's newspaper *The People's Voice* and contributed to other Philadelphia papers.

He retired from the Philadelphia public school system in 1946 and spent nearly a decade "rambling and writing." He then moved to New York where he has spent his time teaching, researching and writing.

Fauset's other works include: articles in *The Crisis*; reviews, articles and short stories in *Opportunity: A Journal of Negro Life;* articles in the *Journal of American Folklore*; *For Freedom* (Philadelphia, 1927), a study of Negro characters written for use in the Philadelphia schools; *Sojourner Truth* (Chapel Hill, 1938), a biography; and with Nellie R. Bright, *America. Red White Black Yellow* (Philadelphia, 1969), a history focusing on parallel racial development in the United States.